KARMIC RECONCILIATION

ALSO BY TORIN M. FINSER

School as a Journey
The Eight-Year Odyssey of a Waldorf Teacher and His Class

School Renewal
A Spiritual Journey for Change

In Search of Ethical Leadership
If not now, when?

Organizational Integrity
How to Apply the Wisdom of the Body
to Develop Healthy Organizations

Silence Is Complicity
A Call to Let Teachers Improve Our Schools
through Action Research—Not NCLB

Initiative
A Rosicrucian Path of Leadership

Finding Your Self
Exercises and Suggestions to Support the Inner Life of the Teacher

A Second Classroom
Parent-Teacher Relationships in a Waldorf School

Education for Nonviolence
The Waldorf Way

The False Door between Life and Death
Supporting Grieving Students, Teachers, and Parents

Leadership Development
Change from the Inside Out

Parables

Guided Self-study
Rudolf Steiner's Path of Spiritual Development

A Call to Teach
Teacher Education and Lifelong Learning

Listening to Our Teachers
Advocacy through Research

KARMIC RECONCILIATION

Clearing a Path for Destiny

*A Workbook for Spiritual-Scientific Study
with Excerpts from Works by Rudolf Steiner*

Torin M. Finser, PhD

SteinerBooks :: 2026

2026
SteinerBooks
An imprint of Anthroposophic Press, Inc.
1 Taconic Place, Ghent, New York 12075
www.steinerbooks.org

Copyright © 2026 by Torin M. Finser. All rights reserved. No part of this book may be reproduced, stored in a retrieval system, or transmitted in any form or by any means, electronic, mechanical, photocopying, recording, or otherwise, without the written permission of SteinerBooks. Excerpts by Rudolf Steiner have been edited for this book. They were previously published and copyrighted by SteinerBooks/Anthroposophic Press. Please see the bibliography for those books.

Cover image: pastel by Karine Munk Finser, Director of Kairos Institute of CfA

LIBRARY OF CONGRESS CONTROL NUMBER: PENDING

ISBN: 978-1-62148-418-9

Table of Contents

Acknowledgments ix
Introduction xi
Unit 1: Karma, Nature and the Forming of Destiny . . . 1
Unit 2: Freedom and Necessity 9
Unit 3: The Great Cosmic Mirror 12
Unit 4: Metamorphosis in the Cosmic Mirror 14
Unit 5: Karma and Heredity 19
Unit 6: Friendships and Karma 22
Unit 7: Humans as the Religion of the Gods 24
Unit 8: Biography 28
Unit 9: Karmic Detective Work 32
Unit 10: More Karmic Links 35
Unit 11: The Moral Crisis of Our Time and
    the Need for a "Grand Reversal" 41
Unit 12: Architecture and Meditation 44
Unit 13: Karmic Adjustment 46
Unit 14: Karmic Physiology 48
Unit 15: Learning to Wait 52
Unit 16: Physiology and Learning to Read Again (Karmically) . 56
Unit 17: Karma and Ethics 60
Unit 18: Letting Go of Evil 62
Unit 19: The Human Life Span and Karma 64
Unit 20: Divine Architects 67
Unit 21: Sleep and Memory 69
Unit 22: Natural Disasters and Those Caused by Humans . . 74
Unit 23: The Universality of Thoughts 77
Unit 24: Our Connection to the Stars 81
Unit 25: Karmic Relationships and Issues of the 21st Century . 83
Unit 26: Intelligence 86
Unit 27: Karmic Restoration 91
Unit 28: Sacredness of Place 94

Unit 29: Looking for Karmic Connections	96
Unit 30: Images of the School of Chartres	100
Unit 31: Karmic Timing	102
Unit 32: Karmic Balance	104
Unit 33: Plato	110
Unit 34: Human Connections	112
Unit 35: Karmic Compensation and How Destiny Takes Shape	117
Unit 36: The Journey after Death	124
Unit 37: Good and Evil	127
Unit 38: Karmic Biography	130
Unit 39: Past and Future Relationships—Moon and Sun	135
Unit 40: Human Encounters	141
Unit 41: The Role of Historical Personalities in the Study of Karma	149
Unit 42: The Age of Michael	153
Unit 43: Planetary Influences in Human Life	155
Unit 44: Unity	159
Unit 45: Where do we belong? Who are our people?	164
Unit 46: Memories	167
Unit 47: Sleep	175
Unit 48: Threefold Humans	182
Unit 49: Tintagel and More	185
Unit 50: Elementals, Karma, and Indigenous Wisdom	188
Unit 51: History through Biography	190
Appendix:	
Our Karmic Companions	193
Threefold Human Nature and World Karma	201
"Thy Will Be Done, on Earth as It Is in Heaven…"	203
Karmic Leadership	204
On Karma (*Steffen Hartmann*)	210
Illness and Karma (*Rudolf Steiner*)	212
The Modern Human Being (*Rudolf Steiner*)	214
Bibliography	215

This book is dedicated to my father

Siegfried E. Finser

with gratitude for our many conversations on karma

Acknowledgments

It gives me great joy to recognize the following friends and colleagues who helped make this book possible:

William Jens Jensen and Chloe Manchester for their superb team effort in editing the manuscript.

John-Scott Legg for agreeing to publish this at SteinerBooks.

Livia in Brazil for the Portuguese translations of *Second Classroom* and *Organizational Integrity*, accompanied by her enthusiastic encouragement to continue writing and speaking on karma.

To Elisa and Unsu in New Zealand for their deep interest in my previous books, steadfast encouragement for this karma project, and generous hospitality over three trips to New Zealand to do leadership development at the Titirangi Steiner School.

To my Center for Anthroposophy colleagues, especially Bev Boyer, Karine Munk Finser, and Douglas Gerwin for their ongoing conversations, support, and sincere interest in my research on karma.

Karmic Reconciliation

"In the Moon sphere, you experience what you did or thought during your earthly life, not as you felt it, but as it has affected the other person. After death, for a period corresponding to a third of one's lifetime, we live through, in reverse order, all that we thought and whatever wrong we did during our earthly lifetime. It is revealed to us by the Moon beings as intense reality...we become aware of how our deeds affected others. And then a strong desire arises within us as spirit human—that what we are now experiencing in the Moon sphere because of our dealings with other people on Earth may again be laid upon us, so that compensation can be made. The resolve to fulfill our destiny in accordance with our earthly deeds and earthly thoughts comes as a wish at the end of the Moon period. And if this wish (which arises from experience of the whole of earthly life back to birth) is devoid of fear, we are ready to be received into the next sphere, the Mercury sphere, into which we then pass.... In this realm we then learn how to shape our future destiny."

(Karmic Relationships, vol. 5, lect. 5)

Introduction

How are we doing as humans on Earth today? Over centuries, many world religions have been founded; beautiful artwork has been created; we continue to marvel at the wonders of nature; and literature and poetry can still lift us to higher dimensions. Yet, there is still so much suffering all around us—international conflicts, marginalization, trauma, income inequality, addictions, and other tragic manifestations. It seems we have thus far made little progress toward the ideals of goodness, beauty, and truth as described by Rudolf Steiner when speaking, for example, about the ideals of Waldorf education. It is astounding to contrast these ideas with what is actually happening in our troubled world today.

Much of what we read and hear about current events is indigestible. I have gone through phases of minimizing my intake of the news. More than ever, when I ingest something troubling, I try consciously to find something else to place in my soul. For example, it was refreshing to find "Good People Everywhere," an online chat group. It seems others are also trying to overcome the negativity and destructiveness in the world around us.

My father pointed out recently that a small number of leaders around the world are causing tremendous pain and suffering to the very people who look to them for help and restitution. He feels that the suffering inflicted on the many by those few in power has great karmic implications, perhaps even more so today than in the past, when many were still held by their common ancestry and traditions. Perhaps the transgressions are even more grievous now that we have arrived at this age of the consciousness soul. We really should know better.

Yet there has also been a growing awareness that so many of the issues that surround us are the outer symptoms of more deeply seated matters. In my consulting work, I was always told to look beyond the "presenting issues." In Waldorf high schools, history teachers are encouraged to work with symptomatology. How can we learn to "read" the events around us as symptoms, as physical manifestation of deeper causes and effects?

This study guide on karmic reconciliation has simmered for many years. As a class teacher, I had a practice of reading anthroposophic literature every night before sleep. I found it helped me ask the spiritual worlds for assistance overnight. Then, when I assumed the role of teacher educator at Antioch University in 1990, I read all eight volumes on Waldorf education again, this time because I found they helped me work with some of the riddles of the adults finding their way toward Waldorf education. Then finally, in the past three years I embarked on a third "round" of study, this time drawing forth passages that I felt would be particularly helpful for the time in which we live.

I have also been asked recently to give short online seminars in the Kairos program offered by the Center for Anthroposophy (CfA), as well as snippets in our CfA leadership training. In June 2025, at an Association of Waldorf Schools of North America (AWSNA) conference in Toronto, I led workshops on Karmic Considerations in Leadership. Now I feel this work has reached the stage at which I would like to offer it as a study guide for groups, schools, and communities that seek to delve more deeply into some of the riddles of the human encounter.

If human beings do in fact experience reincarnation, and if past lives do matter, could it be that some of the symptoms, some of the presenting issues, are connected to longstanding karmic threads that extend far back in time? Just as Resmaa Menakem speaks of traumatized racism held in the "body" over generations, so perhaps the anthroposophic study of karma on a spiritual level can help us unlock some of the root causes of our social struggles.

Over the years, I have identified several key themes that can form a foundation for understanding karma. Before the reader works through this guided self-study, it might be helpful to consider a few signposts prior to starting the fifty-one units that follow:

A. Behind the visible is a less visible world that is every bit as real. Many teachers can recall introducing a class play performance. There is that pivotal moment when one steps out in front of the stage curtain to welcome excited parents and friends, as well as to share a few words about the dramatic production about to take place. Although the audience (usually) does not notice, behind the curtain I often heard students whispering last minute instructions to each other, the scrape of a chair or other props, and the hushed admonition to get ready for the opening scene. All I could do was smile and hope that when the curtain opened in a few seconds, all would be well (and it almost always was). This moment in time reflects the larger stage of karma; there is the "here and now" in front of the curtain, and then all that has taken place and continues behind the curtain. The two are barely separated at times,

and it is well worth our while to consider both the visible and not so visible in the world around us.
B. Intentionality matters. We seek out life situations based largely on circumstances we helped create in the past. The study of karma can help us identify our intentions, work with them, and bring new guidance to future human encounters. Much of what happens in life (even the challenging situations) is the result of our own intentions. We have helped to build, or at least furnish, the house in which we live.
C. Following the preceding law, we seek to compensate for past actions. Due to planetary influences and pre-birth experiences, we come into life well aware of the compensatory actions and encounters needed to bring healing. Many of our schools are karmic communities, serving as a gathering place for individuals who need to do further work together.
D. As part of this work, we seek rebalancing through reincarnation. Whatever is painful, even hurtful, in one life has to be processed in the journey between death and rebirth (in the stage Steiner calls the Mercury sphere). The return to the Earth is an opportunity for compensation in the larger spiritual sense, a chance to rebalance thanks to the experiences learned between lives.
E. Karmic work is transformative. Many of the historical personalities Rudolf Steiner shares in the following pages exemplify transformative work from one life to another. There are even soul-physical transformations in which what was carried as an inner experience then manifests in the next physical body, and vice versa.

F. Karma studies show how we are interconnected. We tend to reincarnate in the same groups (with some exceptions), and we often "find one another" again and again to continue those relationships.
G. When taken up consciously, we can make karmic "adjustments." Just as a chiropractor can adjust the physical body, so we can make adjustments in the soul-spiritual realm for the good of our own health, our work on Earth, and the organizations we serve.

The preceding represents only a brief outline of the core principles behind the study of karma, which are needed more than ever today. We are experiencing on every side the dangers of increased fragmentation of human soul forces. Thinking, feeling, and willing are becoming increasingly separate and disassociated. Outer examples are plentiful—a teacher goes "rogue" and disregards norms and appropriate standards in the classroom; faculty/staff discuss one thing in meetings and then have multiple interpretations afterward, becoming "free agents, acting according to personalized interpretations, with a general lack of follow-through." We cannot solve the issues in our organizations just by creating new policies and HR guidelines (though perhaps also necessary); we need to dig deeper and see why conflicts arise, and why people cannot agree or stick to agreements once they have been articulated. We cannot just look at what's in front of the curtain when so much is happening on the "stage" of repeated Earth lives!

Karma as reconciliation

What does reconciliation mean? Reconciliation is not the same as rectifying. It is more about *coming to terms with*.

You cannot fix it—it is always there. One cannot go backward, but can change the path forward if there is a reconciliation. Knowledge is powerful. *Know thyself!* When you know something, you can relate to it differently. If we look into our past, we can see that we have done some terrible things to one another—trauma upon trauma—all of which lives on in the psyche of humanity and within each of us individually. Karma knits us together; it makes up some of the fabric of our community lives. If we had no community life, there would be no karma. If I were the only person in the world, I would not have any karma. Because there are other people in the world, we do have karma. We evolve in relation to others. Evolving allows us to reconcile.

What matters most is what we do with what we are given

In his 2022 pamphlet on karma, Jens Erdmann describes two kitchens. One is basic, perhaps totally antiquated—an old oven, roughly hewn counters, a simple sink to hand-wash utensils, limited cooking tools, and so on. The other is state-of-the-art, with all the latest gadgets and appliances. Each has its own cook assigned to make a meal. Which will produce better food? The outcome depends on what each cook does in the kitchen and the capacities and skills brought to the art of cooking. So it is with karma; we cannot determine what we are given, but *what matters most is what we do with what we are given.*

Karmic reconciliation is all about what we do in the kitchen of life. This book is meant to aid the reader's engagement in this process. By working with the units in the book and contemplating the assignments, the goal is to illuminate strands from the past—our own as well as the tapestry we share with others. To the extent that we can do this work, we can lift our level of interaction with others from reactive behaviors to more enlightened, mindful, heart-centered responses. The hope for this study guide is that more and more people will engage in these karma studies and that, collectively, we will be able to resolve karmic knots that impede our social life.

Yet, we need help beyond what we can see on a daily basis

For the facilitator of karma studies, what stands in the background behind this much-needed work? All the hierarchies (as articulated by Rudolf Steiner in many books such as *An Outline of Esoteric Science*) have sacrificed to make humans possible. They give everything they can, but living life remains a struggle. Humans have demonstrated a great capacity to inflict harm on one another, to oppress, to commit violent acts. The old order has not worked, and the plea for help has only grown stronger. From the vantage point of Christianity, Christ was sent to help human beings rise and eventually rejoin the hierarchies on a whole new level. If the facilitator of karma has Christ in the background, it will be potent. Other spiritual practices have been given to humanity to help bring change from the inside out, to lift us. As humans, we are now at a stage where we need to do the work, each of us individually. Our meditative life informs everything we do. The devoutness of those observing the Jewish faith, the path of Allah, the way of the Sufi, or other spiritual opportunities can make much difference in creating the soul conditions for karmic reconciliation. In fact, it is precisely in regard to world religions that much karmic reconciliation is needed.

Overview of my methods in this study guide

My attempt is to provide a working text so that the reader can actively engage, not just read the words. Unit by unit, key concepts and insights from Rudolf Steiner are shared in small portions so that one can frequently pause and digest. To assist in the inner processing, assignments are given in each unit—sometimes just topics to contemplate, sometimes to journal quietly, or, if appropriate, to discuss in a group. The reasons for this methodology are manifold:

1. To engage the human soul when it relates to the material in an active way. Steiner often said (for example, in chapter 4 of *An Outline of Esoteric Science*) that even if one has not yet achieved the ability to perceive the akashic record directly, one can gain understanding of spiritual insights through common-sense application by building connections, and by relating things to one's own lived experiences. We need to make the material our own.

2. Grasping ideas only with the intellect can perpetuate many of the injustices inflicted among humans in past centuries and continuing in the world around us. To move truly into the consciousness-soul era, people need to work with more intentionality and give more direction to daily practices. One way for this to happen is to engage the higher stages of the will, especially wish, intention, and resolve (*The Foundations of Human Experience*, ch. 4). We are in charge of what we say and do.

3. The world today needs people who can exercise their conscience. Thus, the titles I have chosen for the units often touch on contemporary social issues. The notion of karmic reconciliation is all about working through the past and validating the basic soul capacity we call *conscience*:

to look inward with tenderness, to accept our role in past events, and to devote healing modalities makes it possible to resolve past issues and prepare for the destiny impulses coming toward us from the future.

4. Steiner said, as mentioned by Liane Collot d'Herbois (1907–1999) in *Meeting with the Therapists* (unpublished, edited): Do not hurry. What matters is that you strengthen your capacity for picture-making/imagination—that you learn to see in pictures in imaginations, and that you learn to read Rudolf Steiner's lectures in your imagination. He said we should see what he is saying and make notes of what we are seeing. Pause, reflect, picture, and even dream!

A note about quotations: Given our present-day values, when Steiner uses the term *man,* I have usually changed it to human beings, and the use of the pronoun *him* I have changed to him/her/they as I felt appropriate, even when in a direct quote. Our language is also in constant need of transformation (and reconciliation around issues of gender).

So please read this book with a pen in hand and a journal on your lap! It is your journey. It is not just about gaining knowledge, but also improving oneself and serving the world with new capacities.

Finally, an invitation

If needed or wanted, I am prepared to meet with individuals, groups and organizations to work on one or more of the units that follow. An introductory session could be held online with Zoom. In the years immediately following the publication of this study guide, I hope to follow up with in-person workshops with schools and groups that are facing challenges that might be helped by some karmic reconciliation. My plan is to harvest some of these field experiences (over several years) to then write an addendum to this book. The hope is to go beyond study to some live, action research on karma!

Unit 1:
Karma, Nature and the Forming of Destiny

Karmic Relationships, vol. 1, lectures 1 and 2

Assignment to prepare: Adopt, find for observation purposes:

1. A stone or crystal
2. A plant (can be an ordinary house plant)
3. An animal/pet or a photo of one that has been part of your life
4. Photo of yourself

> **Exercise:** spend time observing each one as preparation for the thoughts that follow

Karma and Nature

Causes and effects vary in terms of domain:

A. *Lifeless nature, mineral kingdom*—is self-contained, has clear boundaries, causes and effects exist within the same realm. Example of human corpse after death—lifeless body returns to mineral kingdom.

B. *Plant Kingdom and realm of living things*—needs sun, rain, and the whole universe of etheric forces—causes are outside of the effects (results) we see in plants. These same forces also work in humans as an etheric body. After death, the human etheric body continues to expand for a few days and then loses itself into the cosmic etheric, the place from which the etheric forces can then return to nourish plants.

Causative forces work quickly with the Earth forces, often simultaneously. "In review, the mineral kingdom has a simultaneity of causes with the physical, while the plant kingdom has a simultaneity of causes in both the physical and superphysical."

C. *Animal kingdom*—need to look back before creatures' life began to find causes, the origin of species.

Animal kingdom: past superphysical causes for present effects manifest in forms, sensations of animals.

D. *What about human beings?* If we were only physical, we would be like a crystal; if only etheric, we would be like a plant; if only astral, we would be like an animal. But humans also have one more key aspect: the "I," the higher self.

What about the origin of "causes" for humans?

As with the point and line in projective geometry, we need to go out in space and time to find origins—so far out that we find a previous manifestation in the physical in a last life. We need to go backward in time to a former life on Earth to find the causes.

Humans: past physical causes corresponding to present effects in the physical.

Continuation of karma and nature

Influences on human beings from various sources:

1. The mineral realm mostly influences us through the senses: we see, hear, perceive warmth etc. However, our actual relation to the mineral realm is slight. In fact, the brain itself floats in cerebrospinal fluid, thus diminishing the

influence of earthly gravity. **"The organ of our thought is first relieved of earthly weight"** (vol. I, p. 29). As human beings we can move about in the mineral realm freely and independently.

2. It is quite different with the plants. Like nature, humans are influenced by the surrounding life forces; they affect how we grow.

   "What pours in from the wide ether spaces, causing plants to grow, works in us human beings, too, bringing about the original and native predisposition of each one of us, and this has very much indeed to do with our destiny" (vol. I, p. 31).

   We usually only see the outer aspects of it all, but in fact it belongs very deeply to a person's fate if one has formed the organs, such as liver, lung or brain, under the influence of specific nature forces in a particular geographic area of the Earth. **"[Our] nature karma...depends upon the way our ether-body compounds the living fluids in us, making us grow short or tall and so forth..."** (vol. I, p. 32).

   Thus, one part of our destiny or karma has to do with our internal constitution, our wellbeing, comfort, discomfort, contentedness in life. This inner constitution has to do with our ether body, influenced by the life forces around us (and the third hierarchy).

> **Assignment:** After finishing the preceding study on the mineral realm and doing plant observation, one could do some preliminary research on plant forms, particularly on areas of the Earth—desert, mountains, jungle, and so on—to learn how to characterize etheric forces at work.

3. **Assignment on Animals:** Why do elephants live in some geographic areas of the Earth and not others? "Elephant-creating forces" work down to the Earth in certain regions, and influence humans, though not outwardly as with elephants but in shaping the human astral body. Just as sense of wellbeing depends on the plant nature of the Earth, so the sympathies and antipathies in the astral body are influenced by the animal-forming forces. Each person has different sympathies for certain things and antipathies (even prejudice) regarding others. There are hundreds, even thousands of manifestations of sympathies and antipathies that correspond to animal forms but these often reside in the subconsciousness of the human being.

    "And, after all, it is through these sympathies and antipathies that many other things are brought into our life, belonging to our destiny in a far wider sense than the sympathies and antipathies themselves. One person is carried into far distances by his/her sympathies and antipathies. One lives in this or that part of the world because one's sympathies have taken that person there, and in that distant land, the detailed events of one's destiny will now unfold" (vol. 1, p. 35).

> **Assignment:** Do a destiny travel log—where have you been and how has it influenced your life? Describe how you were drawn to that place and what repelled you if anything (sympathies and antipathies). Then characterize what came to you as a result of living there that may have helped shape your destiny path?

Sympathies and antipathies are deeply involved in our human destiny, influenced by the second hierarchy (exusiai, dynamis, kyriotetes), which works with particular strength in the animal kingdom. We communicate with these beings between death and a new birth, which influences what we bring with us from the spiritual world into our next physical existence.

Before we seek out our parents and any inherited hereditary characteristics, a person must first unfold sympathies or antipathies for these characteristics of father and mother. It is not just a matter of physical heredity, but of sympathy for their characteristics.

They give us our innermost stamp and build destiny from our pre-earthly journey.

"Formed in the life between death and a new birth... our sympathies and antipathies enable us to find in life the human beings with whom we must now continue living, according to our former lives on Earth" (vol. 1, p. 37).

Steiner adds an enigmatic statement at the end of the above passage—that, of course, errors and aberrations occur in our acquisition of these sympathies and antipathies and must be balanced out again in the course of destiny through many lives on Earth.

Summary

Physical nature—realm of freedom when we move about in relation to minerals, which influence us through the senses

First constituent of karma—wellbeing or inner comfort or discomfort via the etheric (plants)

Second constituent of karma—sympathies and antipathies via the astral (animals)

Human destiny

This is the most important of all aspects for our destiny, because it involves "living together." Our life is guided from the other side with far greater wisdom than we know. Example: we might meet someone who becomes important in our life. One might ask: How did I come to the moment of meeting this person? It then seems that every step in life, thus far, was along a pathway to meeting that person at the right moment. As we ponder further, it soon appears that there were a whole series of events (also involving many other people) that made it possible to meet—a working of many complexities too great to comprehend! Yet the actual meeting with that significant person in the end had deep significance for our destiny or karma.

When such a decisive event/meeting approaches us, it is often in the unconscious. Yet there is a power in the story line leading up to the meeting that can be compared to a force of nature.

Summary

Third hierarchy (archai, archangeloi, angeloi):
    wellbeing: etheric
Second hierarchy (exusiai, dynamis, kyriotetes}:
    sympathies and antipathies: astral
First hierarchy (seraphim, cherubim, thrones):
    events and experiences: "I"

"What is lived out in this sphere lives out in our true "I," in our "I"-organization, and it lives over from an earlier earthly life" (vol. 1, p. 40). "When you harm someone or help another human being, this entails meeting that person again in the next life to balance out the deed. In the life between death and rebirth, beings are needed who can transmute or metamorphose moral deeds into world-deeds, cosmic deeds" (vol. 1, p. 41). These are the beings of the first hierarchy; they work on the lived events and experiences in human life.

> **Assignment:** Discuss what has been said thus far.

Review and summary

There are three fundamental elements of our karma—our inner constitution, our sympathies and antipathies, and the actual events and experiences in our external life.

So how do the events of destiny evolve out of these three aspects? We are influenced by all three of the above aspects: born to specific parents and at a certain spot on the Earth, in a particular nation, receiving a particular form of education—these are givens that greatly influence our destiny and our life path, particularly our inner constitution and our sympathies and antipathies.

Then there are the events that take place in life: an illness, an accident, a helping hand from a mentor, an earthquake, or a sociopolitical event—these influence us, too.

Assignment: Prepare a discussion on freedom and necessity. How do we work with both dynamics? We are freest in the material realm, but the preceding three steps form us with a strong guidance, the necessity of which we cannot ignore. We are free to work with situations as opportunities. We are most free in our thinking, somewhat in our feeling, but least free in our will which is highly guided by the three destiny influences. The mineral kingdom is the most separated from the gods and thus we are freest there, especially at the moment of death when we set aside the corpse. Our task in life is to learn to place our sensations, thoughts, feelings, and will impulses into the correct relation to the world around us.

Unit 2:
Freedom and Necessity

Karmic Relationships, vol. 1, lecture 3

In our earthly lives, we often feel cut off from the spiritual world; our physical body restricts us to the senses and intellect. Likewise, between death and rebirth we live in the spiritual world which seems remote from the physical world.

When on the Earth, many people are afraid of death, because they live in uncertainty about it. On the other hand, in the life between death and rebirth, people are excessively certain about the earthly life—so much so that it is stunning, makes one faint, which creates a great longing to return to Earth again (vol. 1, p. 47).

It is hard to communicate between the two worlds—soon after death, nouns become absolute gaps in the dead person's perceptions of the earthly world. A person can understand only verbs, the words of time. The materialism of nouns is left behind, and the activity of verbs remains.

As we look back at evolution, the differences between earthly and spiritual perception shrink until a point where the two states of existence are similar.

Are we free, or are we bound completely by karmic necessity?

Imagine building a house for yourself. Once finished, are you still free? Yes, one could sell it or never even move in. For the most part, however, those who build themselves a house move in—and one still remains free to do as one wishes inside the house.

"Likewise in a single human life, in spite of karmic necessity, there are countless things at your free disposal, far more than in a house—countless things fully and really in the domain of your freedom" (vol. 1, p 53).

> **Assignment:** Discuss freedom and necessity in everyday life.

With ordinary earthly consciousness, we live in a realm of freedom, just as fish live in water and are able to move freely. However, when we return to the spiritual world after death, we begin to perceive the impulses that live as karmic necessity. Then we can look back on life and see how we built up what now confronts us as past good or harmful deeds and interactions. *These become one's own, self-initiated karmic necessity.*

Here is another comparison to the same point: "As human beings we walk. But the ground on which we walk is also there. No one feels embarrassed in walking because the ground is there beneath us. One must know that if the ground were not there, one could not walk at all; one would fall through at every step. So it is with our freedom; it needs the ground of necessity. It must rise out of a given foundation. And this foundation—it is really we ourselves!" (vol. 1, p. 57).

We must learn to "read" in our personal karma the tasks for our present life and follow through on what has been carried forward from previous lives. We would be unfree if we did not fulfill the tasks allotted during our last lives. By beholding what was experienced in past lives while on the journey between death and rebirth, we can now direct our destiny to what is reasonable and to what corresponds to prior deeds. We become free not through avoidance but by moving into the "house" we built for ourselves.

Unit 3:
The Great Cosmic Mirror

Karmic Relationships, vol. 1, lecture 4

During the passage between death and a new birth, we come into relation with those whom we were connected to on the Earth. In this passage, a wonderful "reflection" occurs. We see ourselves reflected everywhere in the souls that surround us. Both good and evil deeds are mirrored back to us. We have a feeling: **"This human being you helped. All that you experienced in helping him, all that you felt for this soul, the feelings that led you on to act thus helpfully toward him, your own inner experiences during the deed that helped him, are coming back to you now from his soul"** (vol. 1, p. 63). They are mirrored back to you from the other's soul! (It's the same of course, for one who did harm to another person while on Earth.)

"On Earth, your 'I' was in the body—as it were, a point. Between death and a new birth, it is mirrored to you from the surrounding circumference. This life is an intimate togetherness with the other human souls—according to the relations you have entered into with them" (vol. 1, p. 63).

> **Assignment:** Projective geometry exercise. If possible, seek out a Waldorf projective geometry teacher for exercises involving point and periphery.

Then, in the last third of the life between death and rebirth we form our astral body out of these mirrored images. We carry in our astral body what we have absorbed in the spiritual journey according to the way our actions from the former life were mirrored in other souls. **"This gives us the impulses which impel us toward or away from the human souls with whom we are born again in the physical body"** (vol. 1, p. 64).

Unit 4:
Metamorphosis in the Cosmic Mirror

Karmic Relationships, vol. 1, lecture 4

If in one earthly life, a person does many things warmed through and through by love, these deeds remain as a real force in one's soul. Then, in the spiritual world after death, all of this is reflected back to us as images, and we form our astral body accordingly in preparation for our next life on Earth. This manifests in the next life as experiences of joy and gladness. The love we developed toward a person in one life flows back as joy coming from other human beings toward us. The karmic result of love in one life results in inner warmth and joy in the next.

Then, in the next journey between death and rebirth, those interactions with others on Earth are mirrored back and once again help shape the astral body for the next life. What is the outcome in this third life? The joy and warmth toward others is transformed into a deep interest in others and a delight in understanding the world and other human beings. In this third round, one has a free mind and an open sense toward all that the world has to offer.

Love leads to joy, which leads to deep interest.

By contrast, if one goes through a lifetime mostly following the call of duty, especially a rigid concept of duty, one does not call forth joy in the next life. For example, showing up for a nine to five job that is carried out of financial needs without enthusiasm. As a result of what is mirrored in the journey between death and rebirth, the astral body is shaped in such a way that in the next life **"You feel that people are more or less indifferent to you"** (vol. 1, p. 67). In the third life, such indifference can lead to an astral body whereby **"a person does not know what to do with oneself"** (p. 67). This can include choice of college courses, later career, where to live, and so on.

> **Assignment:** Make a list of things you have done lately out of a sense of duty and things that were done out of love.

Another sequence demonstrating transformation over multiple lives: As another example, let us imagine a person who has harmed someone else out of hatred or antipathy. This can assume a wide variety of forms, from outright criminality to merely criticizing—remember, **"to be a critic, you must always hate a little..."** (vol. 1, p. 68). Following the journey between death and rebirth and the mirroring that occurs, hatred from the earlier life becomes pain, distress, and unhappiness from the world around us—in other words, the opposite of joy. Suffering and pain in the world are often connected to hatred in a previous life.

Someone might object, saying: I cannot imagine being such a bad person that I caused all this sorrow and pain to come to me. We tend to consciously suggest away the antipathies we feel toward others. **"People go through the world with far more hatred than they think—far more antipathy.... Hatred gives satisfaction to the soul... it is not at first experienced in consciousness. It is eclipsed by the satisfaction it gives. But** when it returns as pain and suffering that comes to us from outside, it is no longer so; we notice the suffering quickly enough" (vol. 1, p. 68).

Steiner then says that, of course, there is also "original sorrow" in the present life, sorrow which we did not cause yet nevertheless is carried over from a previous life.

But much sorrow comes from hatred. Then, after another journey in the spiritual world and the mirroring, we return with a kind of mental dullness (compared to the quick, open-minded insight of the love–joy cycle). This quality is a kind of phlegmatic indifference, an obtuseness of spirit, caused by the suffering in a former life.

> **Summary:** Hatred becomes suffering becomes stupidity.

These sequences should help us develop a *will for the future*—a wish to become ever freer and more conscious in what we do and in how we do it.

We can take steps to help. For example, a teacher can help a student who is not very bright or has little talent, which might come from their experience of hatred in a former life. Since some of those to whom the hatred has been directed might again be in the child's environment in this life, a teacher can help:

"Then you will do something as educator so that this child will develop a special love toward those for whom the individual felt specific hatred in former lives on Earth. You will soon see the beneficial result of a love thus specifically roused and directed. The child's intelligence, nay, the whole life of that soul, will brighten.... *Destiny has brought these children together in one class.... As educators they will be able to perceive the wonderful karmic threads that are woven between the one child and the other, as a result of their former lives"* (vol. 1, p. 71, italics TF).

> *Assignment:* We often speak of looping, which is class-teacher-centric. Far more important is that we work with the continuity of the children among each other over many years so they have opportunities to work through their own karmic connections. Have you ever experienced a group of children that seemed to be a karmic community?

Karma is like a stream

A river runs its course and is held by the banks on either side, yet over time can alter its direction. Likewise, with karma we have both self-created necessity and freedom to affect the course of a life on Earth.

Even without knowing the laws of karma, there are many parents and teachers who instinctively know how to help a child who is struggling with learning. Developing love of a subject and of other children in a group can help change the course of schooling by touching into the other "stream" that balances and heals:

Love → joy → open heart
Antipathy and hatred → suffering → stupidity

We tend to reincarnate with the same "contemporaries"—finding one another again through life after life in a rhythmic pattern—A-stream or B-stream (p. 73). We come to Earth in "shifts," each time returning to Earth within the same circle of people. Why?

In a rare personal comment by Steiner, this concept **"has caused me the greatest imaginable pain"** (vol. 1, p. 73).

There are people we read about in history whom we would love to have known personally, but we cannot break out of our karmic cycle to be with them as contemporaries on Earth. Steiner would have loved to know Goethe, for instance. In other cases, we are spared from knowing certain people. Karmic rhythms are powerful streams of human interaction.

Unit 5:
Karma and Heredity

Karmic Relationships, vol. 1, lecture 5

We receive from our parents something like a "model" of our human form and body that predominates during the first six to seven years of life.

In early times, humans could shape their own physical form entirely on their own, but then we **"fell prey to the luciferic and ahrimanic influences... and thereby lost the faculty, out of his own nature, to build his physical body. Humans were not strong enough anymore and needed a model to help. Therefore, we must take it from heredity. This way of obtaining the physical body is the result of inherited sin"** (vol. 1, p. 80).

> **Assignment:** Reflect on heredity as atonement—much of what we struggle with in life, especially in the early years, is a wish to overcome "the given," the hereditary influences of parents, and form our own body, find our own relationships, and our own destiny.

Birth to age seven: strong influence of heredity
After age seven: gradual emancipation
Change of teeth: a physical manifestation of transforming heredity to suit one's individuality

Some people have stronger inner forces as a result of former lives on Earth and need to rely less on the model from heredity. But we all need to transform what we are given, especially during the years between the change of teeth and puberty. And we need help. "This is precisely the task of school. If it is a true school, it should bring to unfoldment in the human being what he/she has brought with them from spiritual worlds into this physical life on Earth" (vol. 1, p. 80).

> **Assignment:** Discuss or journal about the idea that school, and especially teachers, are karmic midwives who help children transform hereditary influences and more fully claim individual destiny.

During the first seven years of life, there is a conflict between the model given by parents and the child's pre-earthly intentions as an individual. This spiritual struggle in a child is expressed outwardly as **"typical diseases of childhood"** (vol. 1, p. 81).

If we are not fully successful in overcoming the model in childhood, illness can occur later on in life. Or, suddenly, at age twenty-eight or twenty-nine, one might feel inwardly roused to strike out on the new path.

> **Assignment:** Reflect on how illness can be an opportunity to bring resolution to conflicting influences vs. contemporary culture which seeks to avoid any form of illness at all costs, focusing on instant suppression and medication. If possible, bring this into conversation with someone else.

If successful in working through the model in the first seven years, the child's relationship to parents evolves from a physical, hereditary relationship to **"an ethical, soul relationship"** (vol. 1, p. 84).

Some people are extremely interested in everything surrounding them; others are not. Some travelers stop everywhere to marvel at all that surrounds them, and others hurry to reach the itinerary's monuments.

Steiner said that human beings who are **"bursting with health"** had a keen interest in the visible world during a former incarnation. In contrast, those who never take an interest in the beauty of stars, art, or nature—those who are indifferent—tend to come back in the next incarnation as "limp and flabby," not particularly healthy. Lack of interest in music, for example, can tend toward asthmatic troubles/lung issues in the next life.

> **Assignment:** What does it mean for our time that so many Covid-19 issues have had to do with breathing and the lungs?

Key concept: *The quality of soul life in one earthly life is expressed in our physical body in a transformed way in the next. Through karma, what was inner becomes outer.*

> **Assignment:** What are the implications for education? How do you see the Waldorf curriculum in light of "soul interest"—Waldorf education for health?

We see that illness and health can be connected to karma. But Steiner adds that not *all* health issues are; there is also karma **"in the process of becoming"**—i.e., we create new karma in each life as we go.

Unit 6:
Friendships and Karma

Karmic Relationships, vol. 1, lecture 6

Sometimes in life, two people have a falling-out whereby a friendship can be abruptly broken—in youth, for example. Two young people are good friends and suddenly, at age twenty, their friendship is broken. If we go back with our karmic gaze, we often find that they were together as friends in their last life, but often in later years. Why?

In the spiritual world, after a mature-life friendship, they developed a great longing to know each other as young people—what was this person like as a youth? In the spiritual world, they stare fixedly at the possibility of a youthful friendship. Thus, they become childhood friends in the next life.

But why could they not stay together in their next life? Why was that friendship broken at twenty years of age?

For Steiner, the mature friendship of the former life was tending toward "selfishness," and thus had to be rectified with the broken friendship in the next.

In a third incarnation, we often meet people in the middle of our life with whom we were connected at the end or beginning of our last lives.

Thus, our childhood friends were often connected to us at the end of a previous life, and those we met in the middle of life were often known to us early or late in the previous life. This is another karmic law: inverse reflection from one life to another.

Assignment: What are the implications for colleagueship and those we meet in professional settings if some were early or late in the previous life—perhaps former parents or siblings, now become colleagues? Can you think of examples of sibling-like people who are now colleagues? What are the implications of this for school governance? What does the karmic law of "inversion" really mean?

Unit 7:
Humans as the Religion of the Gods

Karmic Relationships, vol. 1, lecture 7

In the sleep–waking cycle, the periods of unconsciousness amount to about a third of one's life span. The nights we sleep through give rise to "I"-consciousness. Likewise with an act of will, our "I" is sleeping in us in these deeds. And it is this "I" that has passed through our former lives:

"That is where karma holds sway, my dear friends. Karma holds sway in our willing. Therein are working and wielding all the impulses from our preceding life on Earth; only they too, even in waking life, are veiled in sleep" (vol. 1, p. 99). When we want to memorize something, we often pace back and forth—movement helps with retention.

Mental pictures come and go, but remain as a memory and descend into our organism (from grey matter in the brain to white matter)—when we remember we look within. Thus, to remember is to perceive anew; memory is perception. With intention, and some effort at times, we can dig down and awaken memory from the will—the kingdom of the unconscious.

Going down into the realm of memory we connect with the third hierarchy of angels, archangels, and archai. The outermost lobes of the brain belong to the Earth, but beneath that we connect to the third hierarchy.

> **Assignment:** Experience your breathing—the alternation of the air from outside coming in and breathing out, connecting to the outside world, then within your own self. Likewise, experience the alternation between one's physical side vs spiritual being, in waking or sleeping. In doing so, we alternate our connection with the third hierarchy.

Third hierarchy: most connected to head organization
    and forming of ideas, perceiving—waking
Second hierarchy: rhythmic system—feeling –dreaming
First hierarchy: motor organization—willing—sleeping

When we journey between death and a new birth, we encounter souls of those who lived with us on Earth but also the spiritual beings of the second hierarchy: **"we work upon all that we felt in our earthly life,"** and then with their help **"elaborate our coming earthly life"** (vol. 1, p. 105). With them, we work out the forming of our inner karma, health and illness, and so on.

But if we look still further "down" from our position in the spiritual world after death, we see the beings of the first hierarchy who are under "necessity to form and mold the counter-images" in their sphere where **"all things are judged; yet not only judged, but also shaped and fashioned"** (p. 107). In our spiritual journey **"we behold what the seraphim, cherubim ,and thrones have experienced through our deeds on Earth"** (vol. 1, p. 107).

So just as we see the vault of the heavens above us in life on Earth, after death we look downward and see ourselves as the mirrored image of our deeds. Then we bring down to Earth in our next life our new faculties, talents, genius or stupidity which all come to us in our next life on Earth as the **"facts of Destiny which meet us from without"** (p. 107).

It is like looking up at the cloudy sky and then, afterward, rain begins to trickle down, and we see the wet fields and trees sprinkled with fine rain. Similarly, we see the results of our spiritual journey after death now sprinkling our next life—**"deeds of the gods in consequence of our own deeds in our last life...now spiritually raining down to become our destiny"** (vol. 1, p. 108).

A significant human encounter, a vocation, or placement in one location of birth on Earth—all that approaches us as outer destiny is the image of what was experienced by gods— gods of the first hierarchy.

These gods have **"an inverse religious faith. They feel their Necessity among humans on Earth—whose creators they are. The aberrations human beings suffer, and the progressions they enjoy, must be balanced and compensated by the gods. Whatever the gods prepared for us as our destiny in a subsequent life, they have lived it before us"** (vol. 1, p. 109).

> **Assignment:** What does it mean that humans are the religion of the gods?

One can speak the Our Father and then do the "Reverse Our Father" from the Fifth Gospel (vol. 1, p. 124):

Amen!
The Evils hold sway,
Witness of Egoity becoming free,
Self-hood Guild through others incurred,
Experienced in the Daily Bread
Wherein the Will of the Heavens does not rule,
In that Man severed himself from Your Kingdom
And forgot your Names,
Ye Fathers in the Heaven.

UNIT 8:
BIOGRAPHY

Karmic Relationships, vol. 1, lectures 7 and 8

Examples of reincarnation: Friedrich Theodor Vischer, Franz Schubert, Eugen Dühring.

When doing a case study, helpful steps include:

1. Physical characteristics of a person in most recent life
2. Soul characteristics, astral
3. Stylistic aspects that reveal personality traits such as gesture or mannerism
4. Special events: a snapshot that shows a larger picture (for example, Schubert at the opera and later at a café (vol. 1, p. 117)

> **Assignment:** In preparation for looking for *destiny connections*, each person in the course "adopts" another person they know to practice the above steps, then shares with a group (without mentioning a name).

Put these first four steps together into one tapestry. For example, with Dühring: "And now take all these factors together: the blindness, the mechanistic bent of mind, the persecution he certainly suffered—for the dismissal from the university was not altogether free from injustice, and indeed countless injustices were done to him during his life.... All these things are connections of destiny which become really interesting only when we study them in the light of karma" (vol. 1, p. 125).

Look at "representative personalities" in history and see how karma works from one incarnation to another. One needs to look for the right "currents" in the series of Earth lives and get rid of any preconceived notions and intellectual judgments. Use a narrative method and learn to look with "unbiased eyes" (vol. 1, p. 129).

> **Assignment:** Do assumptions exercise from WLD program, in *School Renewal,* p. 155, by TF.

Karma is spiritual training in perception. Take, for example, Franz Schubert. In an earlier incarnation as a Moor, he developed a gentle, unassuming, flexible soul that later quickened to life the poetic, dreamlike fantasy in the incarnation of Franz Schubert. Yet as the scene in the coffeehouse after an opera demonstrates, he could also have explosive feelings. These were due to the fierce conflicts he experienced in Castile between the Moors and non-Moorish inhabitants.

The method Steiner used (vol. 1, p. 138) employs an intense involvement in a biography. Sometimes a detail that initially seems unimportant can become ever so revealing as a *symptom of a larger pattern.* A person's character is revealed in one's walking style, the swing of a scimitar, or a characteristic gesture.

Study symptomatology and biography—the historian and novelists Barbara Tuchman has said that biography is the prism of history.

> **Assignment:** Each student selects a biography from history for in-depth study over several months. At the end, share verbally. What impressed you most as essential characteristics? Are there any aspects that can be identified as symptoms of the time in which she or he lived?

Further Aspects of Studying Human Nature through Biography *(lecture 9)*

A bodily peculiarity in one incarnation can "**become a particular trend and attitude of soul in the next**" (vol. 1, p. 143).

We need to pay attention to the particular mannerism of an individual. We need to develop penetrating observation skills when observing human beings.

Often the things that are popular as being "the most important" in a person's life—in terms of the outer biography—are not so helpful in karma studies. The philosophy of Hartman, for example, does not offer clues. It was the knee injury that helped solve the mystery!

Karmic Law of Metamorphosis

The bodily organism of a human being (not the head) becomes, in its form and spiritual content, the head in the next incarnation. "**It is also true that what is of the nature of the *will* in the head works especially into the limbs in the next incarnation**" (p. 150). A lazy thinker in one life will not become a fast runner in the next—the laziness of thinking becomes slowness of limb and vice versa.

"**A metamorphosis, an interchange, takes place between the three members of the human being in passing from one incarnation to another**" (vol. 1, p. 150).

With Hartmann, a sunstroke (head) in one life led in the next life, through metamorphosis, to an infirmity of the knee (body). A battle with an opponent in the blazing sun led to sunstroke, and later the affliction with his knee that meant he could not walk in later life. What happened three lives back that set him up for a sunstroke? The opponent in the Crusades had "**suffered injury and embarrassment in an** earlier incarnation at the hands of this brilliant individuality" (vol. 1, p. 151).

Sequence of incarnations:

1. Verbal contest with a "brilliant" adversary (head)
2. Battle in the sun and sunstroke
3. Knee injury and hours spent sitting as a philosopher—abstract thoughts and long book on the unconscious

Another example of metamorphosis is the Franciscan ascetic who inflicted intense self-torture on his own body, lying for hours at a time in front of the altar, praying and mortifying his flesh.

Rudolf Steiner: "Pain makes one intensely aware of the physical body, because the astral body yearns after the body that is in pain, wants to penetrate it through and through. The effect of this concentration on making the body fit for salvation in the one incarnation was that, in the next, the soul had no desire to be in the body at all" (vol. 1, p. 157).

Unit 9:
Karmic Detective Work

Karmic Relationships, vol. 1, lectures 10 and 12

"The really significant streams run their course *beneath* the surface of ordinary history and in these streams the individualities of the individuals who have worked in one epoch appear again, born into the communities speaking an entirely different language, with altogether different tendencies of thought, yet working still with the same fundamental impulse.... There are people who think that a musician must come again as a musician, a philosopher as a philosopher, a gardener as a gardener, and so forth. By no means is it so. The forces that are carried over from one incarnation into another lie on far deeper levels of the life of soul" (vol. 1, p. 163).

To study karma is to tap into the deep, subterranean currents of soul and transformations of capacities: "When the soul has passed through the gate of death, a certain force of attraction to the regions that were the scene of previous activity always remains: even when through other impulses of destiny there may have been changes, nevertheless the influences continue. It works on, maybe in the form of longing or the like" (vol. 1, p. 168).

So, for example, those living in the Middle East who were deeply influenced by Mohammed will carry thought tendencies into the next life, such as a strict determinism. Thus, we can speak of a reincarnation of ideas. More examples include: Haroun al Raschid returning as Francis Bacon, the Arab commander Tarik returning as Charles Darwin, and Muawiya returning as Woodrow Wilson.

"The very interest that some persons arouse in us will often urge us to find a clue to their life-connections. Once we know how to look for these clues in the right way, we will be able to find them" (vol. 1, p. 173).

Steiner gives a long description of Garibaldi: "The important things to note are these remarkable links of destiny. It is in these links of destiny that we may find our guidance to the karmic connections. For it has not directly to do with a person's freedom or unfreedom that one first sees one's name in print on the occasion of a death-sentence, or finding one's wife through a telescope. Such things are connections of destiny; they take their course alongside what is always present in human beings—in spite of them—their freedom. These are the very things, however—these things of which we may be sure that they are links of destiny—that can give a great stimulus to the practical study of the nature and reality of karma" (vol. 1, p. 179).

In the study of a biography, we need to look out for unusual events, encounters, gestures, and personality traits unique to that person. We need to develop an eye for symptomatology, seeing meaning behind the outer appearances, the world in a grain of sand. Whatever is unique in a person can be a clue to the larger story of life before birth.

> **Assignment:** Go back to the historical biographies you prepared. Can you look again for unique characteristics that might be clues to "links of destiny"? [Note to reader: For further examples from history, read about the lives of Lessing, Lord Byron, and Marie Eugenie Della Grazie.]

Much of modern education can obscure possibilities of seeing karmic clues—one has to look at manifestations of human nature that "reveal themselves, so to speak, *behind him*" (vol. 1, p. 192). Garibaldi is an example: "...when we are able to *see behind a personality*, and can look at what in an earlier Earth life was able to enter the body, but in *this* Earth life, because modern civilization makes the bodies unfit, was *unable to enter the body*—then we can begin to have an idea of what such a personality really is.... One, however, who comes over from other times—bearing a soul filled with great and far-reaching wisdom, so that the soul cannot express itself in the body—can never be estimated with the means afforded by modern civilization by what is done in the body" (p. 193).

A philosopher will not come back as a philosopher, artist as artist. Rather, when a person passes from one life to the next it depends on *what is possible in a particular epoch*. This means we need to know the signature of the time in which a person lives (cultural epoch) and use that as a backdrop in understanding a particular individual. What a person expresses outwardly is only a small fraction of the full story!

Unit 10:
More Karmic Links

Karmic Relationships, vol. 2, lectures 1–4

One's study of karma involves seeing how soul impulses work, "transplanted, as it were, from one earthly life into another so that the fruits of an earlier epoch are carried over to a later one" (vol. 2, p. 11). For example: a counselor to Haroun al Raschid returned in the next life as Amos Comenius, who created an original pedagogy, *Pansophia.* There was active correspondence among followers of Bacon and Comenius (the two who had been connected in previous lives in the Middle East).

An excellent example of how soul impulses work from one life to the next is an adventurer who, upon returning home from battles, found his home and family displaced by a more powerful lord, which forced him to live with his band in the forest and work as a kind of serf for the man who had taken his estate. Resentment grew, year by year. In the next life, he returned as Karl Marx, and the man who had seized his estate returned as Engels.

> **Assignment:** For instructors—tell a story, then ask for reflections of deep-seated attitudes in your life that cannot be explained by the biography of this life—affinities and resentments that live beneath the surface in this life and might originate far back in time.

Leaders and followers: People such as Comenius and Bacon influenced others both on the Earth and in their pre-earthly journeys.

"Biographies generally begin at birth and end at death.... Yet for the real happenings of the world, what a man does after his death is immensely important, notably when he passes on the results of what he did on Earth—translated into the spiritual—to the souls who come down after him. We cannot understand the age that succeeds a given age if we do not observe this side of life" (vol. 2, p. 30).

So, for example, the dead Lord Bacon influenced materialism in others—many attached no value to anything that is not a concrete fact available to the senses.

Example of Conrad Ferdinand Meyer: "...being repelled from something that he was nonetheless doing with all force and devotion out of another impulse in his heart—worked on in such a way that, when he passed through his next earthly life, there ensued a cosmic clouding of his memory. The inner impulse was there, but it no longer coincided with any clear concepts" (vol. 2, p. 36).

> **Assignment:** discuss issues with memory today, which is influenced by many things, including physiology. But could there be a connection with previous life and doing things (jobs) for which we have no enthusiasm?

Recommended reading on a similar subject: Novels *Code to Zero* by Ken Follett, and *Memory Wall* by Anthony Doerr.

Pestalozzi, Emerson, and Grimm (lecture 3)

We need to learn to look at ourselves objectively and with humility, instead of instinctive, emotional impulses rooted in the subconscious that lead to arrogance and pride. We need to use our consciousness to penetrate the hidden sequence of historical events and ways in which we belong to the whole universe. "Recognition of one's place in universal existence invariably invokes humility, never arrogance. All genuine study pursued in Anthroposophy has its ethical side, carrying with it an ethical impulse" (vol. 2, p. 42).

Example of a slave overseer who lived 100 BC:

1. He tried to make life easier for the slaves he supervised, but his boss was a rough, brutal personality who aroused deep animosity in the slaves. The overseer was often forced to obey the owner, though usually unwillingly.
2. In his journey after death, the overseer was surrounded by all the souls with whom he had been connected on Earth, both the slaves and the boss from the previous life.
3. During the ninth century AD, the overseer was again born, but now as a woman who became the wife of the former "boss" owing to their karmic connection (karmic compensation). They lived together on a commune, and the former "boss" had a nominal position whereby he became everyone's servant and frequently received "knocks and abuse" from the commune members. Those members were in fact the former slaves from the previous life, and the former "boss" found himself a **"servant of them all—he had to experience the karmic fulfillment of many things that, through the instrumentality of the overseer, his brutality had inflicted upon those people"** (p. 44). In this incarnation, the woman who had formerly been the unwilling overseer was able to settle any lingering karma with the "boss."
4. This woman then reincarnated again in the eighteenth century, not in a commune made up of the former

slaves, but now as the enthusiastic teacher and leader of a large group of children. He had a passion for helping them through an inspired, new form of education. This remarkable person found karmic fulfillment as a great teacher of the children—the human souls with whom he had been connected during three incarnations. This man is known to us as Johann Heinrich Pestalozzi.

How can we begin to find karmic connections through history?

1. Looking for clues: extensive study of the biography of a person, looking for outstanding characteristics; the more intangible, more intimate traits of a person, their gestures and habitual mannerisms - not so much the *what* but also the *how* a person speaks.
2. Make an artistic inner picture of these characteristics. One has to know the person really well to do so and then **"one finds that it is no longer the mere gesture that one is contemplating, but around the gesture the figure of another human being takes shape"** (vol. 2, p. 47).

> **Note to reader:** Compare and contrast the lives of the following figures expanded upon in the Karmic lectures—Tacitus and his friend, Pliny the Younger; Matilda of Tuscany and her mother Countess Beatrice of Lorraine; Ralph Waldo Emerson and Herman Grimm.

Finding karmic links: "One must first have an impression and then everything crystalizes around it. Thus, we had first to envisage the picture of Herman Grimm opening Emerson's *Representative Men*. Now Herman Grimm used to read in a peculiar manner. He read a passage and then immediately drew back from what he had read: it was a gesture as though he were swallowing what he had read, sentence by sentence. And it was this inner gesture of swallowing sentence by sentence that made it possible to trace Herman Grimm to his earlier incarnation. In the case of Emerson, it was the walking to and fro in front of the open books, as well as the rather still, half-Roman carriage of the man...it was these impressions that led one back from Emerson to Tacitus. Plasticity of vision is needed to follow up on things of this kind" (vol. 2, p. 56).

Difference between birth and death (Lecture 4): "Here on Earth, death is something that breaks in upon us. The descent from the spiritual world (birth) is completely different. It is a matter, then, of fully conscious action, a deliberate decision proceeding from the deepest foundations of the soul. We must realize what a stupendous transformation takes place in the human being when the time comes to exchange the forms of life during pre-earthly existence of the soul and spirit for those of earthly existence. The descent entails adaptation to the prevailing conditions of civilization and culture, as well as to the bodily constitution that a particular epoch is able to provide. Our own epoch does not readily yield bodies (let alone conditions of culture and civilization) in which Initiates can live again as in the past. And when the time approaches for the soul of some former Initiate to use a physical body once again, it is a matter of accepting this body as it is and growing into the environment and the current form of education. But what once was present in this soul is not lost; it is merely expressed in some other way. The basic configuration of the soul remains but assumes a different form" (vol. 2, p. 61).

> **Assignment:** Discuss the following questions.

1. What is the meaning of the contrast—death as something that "breaks in upon" and just happens, whereas birth is a "fully conscious action"?
2. Considering the world today, what are the adaptations to the "prevailing conditions of civilization and culture" that those being born today need?
3. Initiates (and I assume others) have to accept "the body as it is"—what are the implications? Could someone with special needs be a former initiate?
4. We also have to adapt to and accept the "environment and current form of education." What does that mean for those being born today? The work of the soul in a past life is not lost; the basic configuration remains but assumes a different form.
5. How can we then recognize the initiates of the past among us?

Unit 11:
The Moral Crisis of Our Time and the Need for a "Grand Reversal"

Karmic Relationships, vol. 2, lecture 5

We need to recognize that many of our actions have roots in moral causes that we created in past ages. We need to stand in wonder that most things in everyday life are incomprehensible—but that realization is the beginning of a true striving for knowledge. *Wonder* at what is not easy to understand or explain. *Enthusiasm* for seeking deeper meaning in life.

One example of the "grand reversal" from one life to the next is Nero, who did much harm to many people during his reign shortly before the end of the Roman Empire.

"**A life abounding in things of external value reflects itself inwardly in such a way that its bearer** [in the next life] **considers it utterly worthless and commits suicide. The soul becomes sick, half demented, seeking external entanglements... the soul** [in the next life] **becomes directed against itself**" (p. 78). The Nero destiny sheds light on the subsequent Meyerling destiny in the personality of the Austrian Crown Prince Rudolf, who committed suicide. "**We see how this world justice is fulfilled and how the wrong returns, but in such a way that the individual is himself involved in creating the balance. That is what is so stupendous about karma**" (vol. 2, p. 80).

The grand reversal means that we set conditions in one life that require rebalancing in the next. In the case of Nero, harm to others results in harm to oneself.

> **Assignment:** How is this a path of morality? What are the implications for living our lives in the present while aware of our role as causes of future effects? How do we hold the future of good and evil?

The healing available in earlier epochs for outer sensory observation has been lost. As we gaze into nature, we realize that not all the demands of vision are satisfied—hearing, seeing, feeling perceptive processes are unsatisfied (as if we lack adequate food). When we gaze into nature, "**the perceptive faculty in his life of soul deteriorates. He gets a kind of 'consumption'**" (vol. 2, p. 82).

"It was known that the *Temple Architecture*, where people beheld the equipoise between downward-bearing weight and upward-bearing support, or when, as in the East, they beheld forms that were really plastic representations of moral forces when they looked at the architectural forms confronting the eye and the whole of the perceptive process, or experienced the musical element in these forms—it was known that here was the remedy against the consumption that befalls the senses when they merely gaze out into nature. And when the Greeks were led into their temple, where they beheld the pillars, above them the architrave, the inner composition and dynamic of it all, then their gaze was bounded and completed... when one faces a work of great architecture created with the aim of intercepting the vision, rescuing it from the pull of nature" (vol. 2, p. 83).

The foregoing is one aspect in terms of the outer path. Then there is the inner path. If we practice self-knowledge (such as working with surging emotions), one travels an inner path of development: "*...comprehension of the world expressed in imagery and pictures* leads us toward our innermost being. As long as we strive for self-knowledge with abstract ideas and concepts, nothing is achieved. But when we penetrate into the inmost being with pictures that give concrete definition to experiences of soul, then we achieve this aim. The inmost kernel of our being comes within our grasp" (vol. 2, p. 83). We need to meditate in pictures.

Architecture is created by humans to frame and give boundaries to what is no longer possible as pure experience of nature. Architecture frames and balances the soul experience—it humanizes purely sensory experience.

> **Assignment:** What have you experienced recently in "imagery and pictures," whether in nature or art, that awakened wonder in your soul?

Unit 12:
Architecture and Meditation

Karmic Relationships, vol. 2, lecture 5

Outer vision needs architectural forms that overcome raw sensory perception. Inner meditation needs pictures and images to overcome abstract concepts.

Now comes the mysterious aspect: There is an "intermediate domain...if you let *that* work in your life—if you go about with inner self-knowledge deepened through imagination and with sense perceptions made whole and complete through forms created and inspired by a real understanding of human nature—then one's feeling in regard to strokes of destiny will be the same as it was in ancient times. By cultivating the domain between the experience of true architectonic form and the experience of true, symbolic imagery along the path inward, we become sensitive to strokes of destiny. We feel that what befalls us comes from earlier lives on Earth" (vol. 2, p.85).

The Goetheanum building, along with the cultivation of Anthroposophy, is "in itself an education for the vision of karma. And that is what must be introduced into modern civilization: education for the vision of karma" (vol. 2, p. 85).

Unit 12: Architecture and Meditation

> **Assignment:** Discuss how can we begin to understand this. Share a picture of one of your favorite buildings (from history, your travels or your local community). Then have a conversation about the picture. Be mindful that architecture set in nature and images or pictures formed in meditation engage the *etheric formative forces (plastizieren) needed to develop the sense for destiny.*

Karma exercises involve seeing how the impulses, gestures, and soul configuration from one life *form and shape the biography of the next life. The etheric is influenced by the journey between death and a new birth.* The "vision for karma" requires the etheric perception cultivated by the meeting of the two pathways described above—the creative tension in the domain in-between.

Unit 13:
Karmic Adjustment

Karmic Relationships, vol. 2, lecture 6

Anthroposophy can help us take more interest in people and heighten perception so that we can let go of our preoccupation with "self" and enter into the "other." This can be challenging at times, especially when the relationship is part of a "karmic adjustment"—things happen; at times this is disagreeable or painful, but karma is there to help.

"You have done something to another person that calls for a karmic compensation. You go on living with the other person after you have both passed through the portal of death. You live, then, *within the other person*" (vol. 2, p. 90).

A and B live separate lives on the Earth, and then they die. In the spiritual world they confront one another, and now A lives in B and B lives in A (as well as in themselves). "In the spiritual world, we live entirely within one another... you yourself cause all that is to be brought to pass as karmic compensation during the next earthly life by living in the other. It is only on descending again to the physical world that Person A makes what you have put into him/her—*into his or her own deed*. In the next earthly life, that person comes to meet you with what you have actually willed to inflict upon yourself through the other" (vol. 2, p. 91).

This karmic compensation or adjustment comes about because we dwell within one another during the time between death and rebirth.

Assignment: How can we come to know which meetings are a result of "karmic adjustment" or are just things that happen as chance encounters? Are there, in fact, any chance encounters? Or is everything karmic? Either way, what are the implications of karmic adjustment on how we live our daily lives?

Unit 14:
Karmic Physiology

Karmic Relationships, vol. 2, lecture 6

More clues as to how to discover karmic connections:
A person's gestures in performing on stage
Look especially at the hands
Look for characteristic gestures and habits
Then look past the physical—see below

Little remains after death of the head impulses, but that which lives in the rest of the body is often brought to expression in the head in the next life (and vice versa).

When looking at an artist, it is not the reputation that counts, but rather *"what* **exactly he does in his art, how he conducts himself in it—these things are specially determined in karma"** (vol. 2, p. 95).

When we meet someone again, it is not only the moment of meeting that counts. We might need to try and recall any intimate previous experience of the person in a previous meeting that might shed some light: **"We need a fine sense for the intimacies of life... (to) develop the inner mobility of soul needed for a deeper penetration into karmic connections"** (p. 96).

Knowing how a person thinks (when considering karma) is less helpful than learning to know how a person feels.

And for our own self-knowledge, too, we descend into the depths of the soul and perceive **"the inexplicable shades of** feeling that are not caused from without but that arise from the depths within" (vol. 2, p. 97).

> **Assignment:** Journal question. What are your shades of feeling that are not caused from without but arise from the depths within?

If we want to understand karma, we need to *look through* a human being, not just *at* the external, physical aspects but at *the way* a person speaks, thinks, reflects his/her upbringing and experiences. We need to see the essential nature that is "hovering in the air." We need to disregard the action of the hands, arms, legs, and outer experiences of a person, and instead watch their mood or temperament—things in which arms and legs do not take part. We need to look past the purely physical and seek the *transparency* of the human being.

Three stage transparency exercise

1. Look through what is usual activity of arms and legs, make it transparent, and the Moon appears (and all that has to do with phantasy)
2. Think away all that is emotional or sense bound, including the whole rhythmic system. In that transparent place, the Sun-being of yourself emerges
3. Disregard your thoughts, make the head transparent and Saturn emerges in the background

> **Assignments:**
> 1. Practice the E, A, O exercises in eurythmy: (children: Straight as a spear I stand) O away, A away, E away.
> 2. Make the planetary seals as transparencies.

Summary of transparency work:

"So long, however, as you look at your arms and legs, you are not aware of what you fulfil through having arms and legs. You see this only when you no longer look at your arms and legs but find the impulses of the Moon in the activity of arms and legs. Then it is a matter of going a step further and disregarding all that we absorb by means of the senses, what we have in our soul by means of the senses—whether we are practicing the exercise alone or with others. We behold the human being then as Sun being; we see the Sun impulse in the human being. Again, we must disregard the fact that human beings have a certain tendency of thought, a certain tendency of soul—then we realize the human being as a Saturn being" (vol. 2, p. 100).

In all of the foregoing, we need to learn to see the forces that work in place of the physical and ordinary.

Example: "When I do the most trifling thing, when I pick up the chalk here—as long as I merely see this fact—picking-up the chalk—then I know nothing of karma. I must do away with all this. I must bring it about that all this can reproduce itself in a picture, can appear again in a picture. Not in the strength that is contained in my muscles—this explains nothing at all—but in the picture that takes the place of the act appears the force that induces the hand to move in order to pick up the chalk. And it appears as something coming from previous incarnations" (vol. 2, p. 101).

The visible human is replaced by the invisible human, and instead we see Moon, Sun, and Saturn impulses. But this invisible person that emerges is not of the present, but one of the preceding incarnations, or several previous incarnations.

In summary

Take arms and legs away to see Moon forces at work
Take chest/rhythmic/senses away and see Sun forces
Take head and thoughts away and see Saturn forces

Unit 15:
Learning to Wait

Karmic Relationships, vol. 2, lecture 7

Rudolf Steiner worked with Goethe's fairytale, "The Green Snake and the Beautiful Lily," by first reading it in 1889, and then reexperiencing it in 1896, and finally again, in 1903. In this way, he was able to do something with it in connection with writing his mystery dramas. **"We need to be able to wait for the inner experience"** (vol. 2, p. 105).

Real things often demand a waiting time for ripening. We have to be willing to give ourselves time, to wait for experiences to ripen within the soul.

This is contrary to our incessant urge today to save time and do things more quickly. We are smart but not wise.

Three-day karmic exercises

1. Remember something that happened to you earlier in the day or a few days ago. Paint an inner picture: the scene, colors, tone of voice, style of speaking, time of day—work to create that picture in your mind's eye with great precision. Then, during the night, when we are asleep and the physical and etheric body are lying in bed, the astral body will bear the picture you have created and give further shape (outside of the sleeping physical and etheric body). The picture is worked on in the external ether into a more refined picture that can be visualized by the eye

of the spirit. So, in the morning, when we wake up, the astral body stamps this stronger image from the night into the individual human etheric body that has been at rest all night.

2. On the second day, we go about our usual lives, but underneath it all the image is descending into the etheric body. Then in the second night, while the etheric body is at rest and the astral has gone out during sleep, the etheric body further elaborates the picture. It is important that from time to time during the second and subsequent days, we continue to occupy ourselves with the original picture. We need to exert ourselves spiritually to continually re-create the original image—this activity of the soul is good for us!

   On the second day, one may begin to feel that the picture has changed. Our relationship to it and our feelings for it may have begun to change. The picture will begin to transform and then it goes into the next night of sleep.

3. Now in the next day the picture is carried down from the etheric body into the physical body. The image is impressed into the physical, the nerve-senses, and into the blood-processes (vol. 2, p. 110). The physical body "works up the whole picture," and spiritualizes it. There arises a greatly magnified transformation of the picture. When you wake up in the morning of the third day, the picture stands there as a kind of cloud hovering over you.

4. On the fourth day you rise from sleep enveloped by this cloud, and you can experience your will contained in it. You are in it.

Review of steps

1. First day, picture an event or situation—**mental image**
2. Experience the **feeling** conveyed on second day
3. Experience the **will** contained in the picture

> **Assignment:** Do the three-day karmic exercise. Make a descent into all three soul realms over three successive nights, following the order above. Discuss and/or journal the results.

But the will cannot fully express itself in the final stage, it is as if fettered, like a sprinter at the starting gate about to take off, just before the signal to begin in a race. You experience the tremendous potentiality of the will but cannot take off, as you are held in fetters.

"**When this experience of feeling yourself in a pillory develops…with the will fettered through and through, then, if you pay attention to it, you will find that the will begins to transform itself.** *This will becomes sight….* **It becomes an eye of the soul. And the picture, with which one rose from sleep, becomes objective. What it shows is the event from the previous Earth life, or of some previous Earth life, which had been the cause of the experience that we shaped into a picture on the first day**" (vol. 2, p. 112).

Will becomes sight!

1. Thinking/picturing
2. Feeling/transforming
3. Willing/seeing

All this must become a habit of the soul in working through experiences and events in daily life. One then finds an inner continuity. Rather than rush from one thing to another, one has to let things mature within the soul. This inner, active work can help us develop an attitude of soul that we can draw upon when needed and learn to see things in the light of karma.

> **Assignment:** Use an example of something unpleasant that happened to you, a personal encounter you remember vividly from the recent past or just the last day or two. Put yourself back in that situation and build up the picture afresh. Do the three-day exercise. It can help us become free. How? In this life we often encounter the effects of previous experiences in past lives, and we bounce around from one **effect** to the other. If we can get to the "fettered" stage in which we see how this is bound up in the will, we can get a glimpse of the **cause** that has fettered us.

I am the same "I" now that I was then, but I had a quite differently constituted personality in a previous life. The events of the past were stamped into the etheric world or the astral world and I have to go backward to loosen the effects from the causes.

This process fills us with new courage and gives us the ability to confront the things placed before us in life.

> **Assignment:** Ask yourself whether you have gained anything by waiting. What did you experience in doing the three-day exercise?

Unit 16:
Physiology and Learning to Read Again (Karmically)

Karmic Relationships, vol. 2, lectures 7 and 8

In each case, correlations can be observed. There are some people who are **attentive** to everything in life, to whom observing details is important. For example, the professor who delivered focused lectures, and then one day was off. Later, he asked someone in the audience, "Why did you sew on the button that had always been missing?" (vol. 2, p. 121). He used the missing button as a point of concentration.

When one is attentive to things, that person tends to connect, go to them, and become active in the limbs. The whole body is active, as well as the senses. This activity passes over into the structure of the head in the next life. The head develops a strong relationship to the Earth forces. Others take little interest in things around them; awareness ebbs and flows, as if in a dream. In the next life, such individuals become fainthearted; they can become cowards.

Basic karmic truth—the non-head part of a human being of one earthly life transforms into the shaping of the head in the next. "**The head is always the product of the non-head nature of the preceding earthly life. This holds good for the whole concentration of forces in the constitution of the human being**" (vol. 2, p. 121).

Unit 16: Physiology and Learning to Read Again (Karmically)

These things manifest in physiology: The head forces connected to the Earth in one life lend themselves in the next life to heavy, low-set brow; bones that are strongly formed; and hair that grows quickly—all related to powers of attention in previous life. Attentiveness leads to strong bones and muscles, and then, in the next life, a person with courage. *Attentiveness in one life leads to courage in the next.*

Consider this in relation to Waldorf education and self-education of the teacher. "**If we go through our present earthly life with a certain amount of self-knowledge, then we can prepare for the next earthly life. If we drift superficially through life without any real interest in anything, then we can be sure that we will be a coward in our next earthly life. This is because a detached, inattentive character forms few links with its environment. Consequently, the head organization in the next life will lack a relationship to the Earth forces. The bones remain underdeveloped, hair grows slowly.... These things...reveal the connection between the spirit and soul on the one side and the natural-physical on the other. Yes, my dear friends, from the very details of the shape of the head and of the whole structure of the human being, we can as it were look over into the previous earthly life.... For the human being is a *picture of one's previous earthly life*"** (vol. 2, p. 124; italics by TF).

A person who thinks and ponders much in one incarnation tends to return in the next as a thin, delicately made person. But a person who lives a life grasping the outer world tends in the next life to accumulate a good deal of fat. So, there is a connection between the spiritual/moral way a person lives in one life and the physical constitution in the next.

Likewise, when a person thinks a great deal, then in the next life, he/she will have healthy skin. Whereas a person with many freckles or skin issues may not have been a thinker in their past life. **"Matter is the outer revelation of the spiritual"** (vol. 2, p. 126). The human head, the ears, nose, eyes etc. are related to revelations of Imaginations.

> **Assignment:** Read Norbert Glas's chapter on ears, in *Reading the Face: Understanding a Person's Character through Physiognomy*. The chapter also appears in the appendix of Torin Finser's *A Second Classroom: Parent–Teacher Relationships in a Waldorf Classroom*.

When the trunk is longer than the upper part (middle of chest to neck), we have a person who moved quickly toward the midnight hour of the journey after death and then descended slowly back to Earth. This person will require a lot of sleep each night. However, when the trunk is shorter than the upper part of the torso, this person passed slowly from death to the midnight point and then descended quickly back to Earth and a new incarnation. This person will need less sleep.

These correspondences also apply to someone who views things superficially. In the next life, such a person is a sleepyhead. And one who is the opposite of dull—a person who was attentive and active in mind and feelings will have less propensity to sleep in the next life.

"There are human beings who...ascend very high into the spiritual, and there are others who do not rise so high. Those who ascend very high will eat in order to live. Those who do not rise so high will live in order to eat" (vol. 2, p. 129). Observe how people take food at the table and the gestures used to help themselves to food—it is very revealing.

Unit 16: Physiology and Learning to Read Again (Karmically)

Trivial habits in one life can lead to gluttonous habits in the next—what we do in one life affects the next. When a past life works in the right way, those who are able to be serious (even though they can laugh, too) are also able to focus. Someone who lives as if half asleep in one life can become a chatterbox in the next.

The threefold aspect: **"A study of the *head* is an Imaginative process, projected into the sense world; a study of the *rhythmic system* must be truly Inspired, though active in the realm of sensory observation, within the sense world; a study of the *metabolic-limb system must be Intuitive, a suprasensory activity in the sense world"*** (vol. 2, p. 135).

Head system—imaginative ideation
Rhythmic system—continuous mobility of inspirations
Metabolic system—everything that is not suprasensory is expelled to make way for intuition

> **Assignment:** Observe people, both those you know well and those who are relative strangers. Observe proportions, even try to sketch heads or other physical features. Then consider them in light of the thoughts in this unit.

Conduct additional reading on physiology to support this unit—for example, L. F. C. Mees, *Secrets of the Skeleton: Form in Metamorphosis*, how limbs have a little "head," etc.

Unit 17:
Karma and Ethics

Karmic Relationships, vol. 2, lecture 9

After death, human beings live through their sleeping life on Earth backward. For example, if someone lived to be sixty, one third of life, or twenty years, was spent sleeping. When we sleep, we are unconscious, but when we live through our sleeping years after death, in reverse, we are fully aware of what is happening. The impressions on this journey after death are vivid; there is nothing dreamlike about them. It is like a photographic negative... you feel the inverse of what you experienced in life. "**[When] journeying backward after death, you do not feel what *you* experienced during earthly life, but you slip, as it were, into the other person and feel what *that person* experienced as the result of your actions**" (vol. 2, p. 140).

In this backward retrospect after death, the impressions are powerful, intense, and stronger than one would experience on Earth. It is a kind of karmic fulfillment. Why is this so strong? Because after death we set aside the etheric and physical, and the Moon beings draw near and impregnate the pictures with cosmic substance. "**After death, therefore, we pass through the region of the Moon beings, and what we experience as the balancing-out of our own deeds is stamped with great force in the cosmic ether**" (vol. 2, p. 142).

"In this backward journey after death, which lasts for a third of the time of the earthly life, karma is prepared. For the Moon beings mingle in these 'negatives' of one's deeds, including one's deeds in the life of thought. The Moon beings have a good memory, and they inscribe into the cosmic ether every experience they share with a human being. We pass through the life between death and a new birth, and then on the return journey, when we return once more into the Moon sphere, we find everything inscribed there. And we bear it all with us into our life in order to bring it to fulfillment by means of our earthly will" (vol. 2, p. 151).

For example, if we had hit someone, in the journey after death we experience how that person felt when struck.

Aristotle spoke of *being, quantity, quality, relation, position, space, time, possession, action, suffering*. We need to be able to understand his use of this ancient wisdom in manifold permutations (vol. 2, p. 143).

> **Assignment:** How might the backward retrospect after death inform how we live our lives while living on Earth? Can we gradually learn to understand that many of the human encounters we have are part of this "karmic fulfillment"?

Unit 18:
Letting Go of Evil

Karmic Relationships, vol. 2, lecture 10

Spiritual laws are not identical to natural laws, thus there is an abyss between the moral/psychical and the natural/physical. When a human being dies, natural laws of the Earth are left behind and the journey in the spirit realm begins. During our journey through spiritual Sun existence (and the second hierarchy—exusiai, dynamis, and kyriotetes), **"a kindly, gracious welcome is extended to all the good intentions and purposes that were harbored in our life of soul on Earth. This could also be expressed by saying that whatever has lived in a person's soul with any nuance of goodness is received in the Sun existence with graciousness, but the evil is utterly rejected; it cannot enter"** (vol. 2, p. 159). All that is good in a person's soul will be seen as bright as sunlight; all that is evil will be like a spot where no sunlight can penetrate.

In the journey after death, we must leave behind all that is evil at the threshold of the Sun existence. If there is much evil, much is left behind and the journey is shorter, with less time in Sun stage and only the reentry through the Moon stage. A hardened evil-doer will return to the Earth relatively quickly.

The life of procreation is influenced by the Moon stage of the journey, and the head-life is influenced by the Sun.

1. "A part of human beings that has passed through the realm of Sun existence appears on Earth...is the part of the human being that is dependent upon the workings of the head—predisposition to good health."
2. "A part of human beings that has not passed through Sun existence [but just the Moon influence] appears on Earth. It is the part of human beings that is connected with the life of procreation—predisposition to illness" (vol. 2, p. 165).

So, in the next earthly life our spiritual realizations from the journey come to realization in the physical. This is karma.

> **Assignment:** At a time when we see so many examples of evil in the world around us, how can the spiritual laws just described help us?

Unit 19:
The Human Life Span and Karma

Karmic Relationships, vol. 2, lectures 11 and 12

At the beginning of earthly life, the animal nature predominates in human

In the middle, the plant nature predominates.

At the end, the mineral nature predominates

From birth until age thirty-five, the human organism provides up-building support. After thirty-five, as destructive forces grow stronger, we become weaker in connection with native soul forces. See chart: karmic demands in life from ages one to twenty-one, karmic fulfillment from ages twenty-eight to forty-nine.

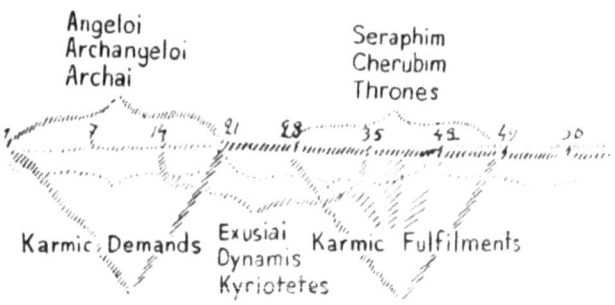

Assignment: Read the article "Karmic Leadership" (from *Renewal Magazine,* fall 2025), in the appendix.

Today there are many people on the Earth whose most recent significant incarnation occurred in the eighth and ninth centuries, when interest in pre-earthly experiences was becoming weaker: "I am here! What went before does not interest me. What does interest me is what follows after death. This is the consciousness that grew stronger and stronger during the first Christian centuries. The feeling for pre-earthly existence grew dim... and that is why intellectual cleverness is now directed entirely toward the earthly" (vol. 2, p. 179).

Compare this to the difference between "front space" and "back space." Eurythmy teachers and those trained in Bothmer—Spacial Dynamics®—with Jaimen McMillan view back space as pre-earthly and front space as what lies ahead of us.

Our intelligence today can reach up to the third hierarchy. People are clever through their education in their first epoch of life. Today we have greatness in intellect. In the second epoch of life, we become capable of procreation, connecting us to the second hierarchy, which reaches downward toward humankind.

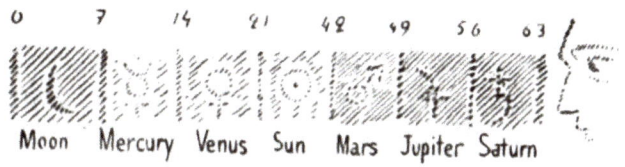

Planets and seven-year phases of life (p. 186)

We go back into planetary spheres after death. There are people whose karma is elaborated mainly in the Mercury sphere, or the Venus sphere, or Sun sphere. This influences our next life on Earth.

Voltaire was strongly influenced by the Mars sphere: "When our gaze is directed to the experiences lived through by this individuality between death and a new birth, before he became Voltaire—experiences that were the outcome of his previous earthly lives—we find that the fruits of his studies in Northern Africa, with their subsequent Cabalistic trend, were wrought out in the sphere of Mars during the second half of his life between death and rebirth. And with the results of the metamorphosis that can be wrought in the Mars-sphere, Voltaire came again in the 18th century as Voltaire. I am therefore able to bring him forward as an example of the elaboration of karma in the sphere of Mars between death and a new birth" (vol. 2, lecture 12).

Jupiter people show the influence of weaving wisdom. Saturn gives a strong influence from the past. Example is Victor Hugo: "In short, this individuality who had once been initiated in the Hibernian Mysteries, was born in our epoch—our epoch in the wider sense—as Victor Hugo. In its romanticism, in its whole configuration, Victor Hugo's life bears the stamp of karma wrought out in the Saturn sphere" (p. 196).

> **Assignment:** Continue working with a biography (see lecture 14, p. 213).

Image to help with next section: Raphael's *Sistine Madonna* with strips of tape over some parts of the glass covering. Of course, you would feel that there is something more to be seen—something left out. It is similar when studying a biography of a historical figure; one senses there is much that is not known. The best sources can be the person's original works—diaries and handwritten notes. People sometimes provide hints of the unseen in biography (karma).

> **Assignment:** Have you experienced biography work? If so, how does this unit supplement it? If not, why do it now?

Unit 20:
Divine Architects

Karmic Relationships, vol. 2, lecture 13

The following chart shows how things are constituted with a=physical, e=etheric, c=astral (vol. 2, p. 199):

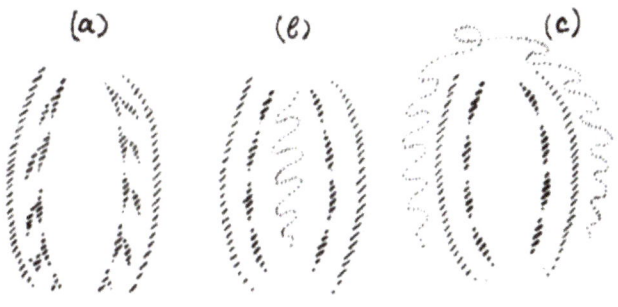

"When the gods desire cosmic vision, they gaze through the eye of the Moon. But when they desire to behold the cosmos from the Earth... then they must look from out of the human being. Humans are the other eye of the gods!" (vol. 2, p. 204).

"What we do with our everyday consciousness, the intentions we form, and so forth—all this depends upon ourselves; but our karma is shaped and fashioned by the Hierarchies within us. They are the architects and shapers of an entirely different world order—a world order belonging to the soul, the moral sphere of life" (vol. 2, p. 205).

Countless divine beings take part in shaping human karma:

1. In our thoughts we share in the life of the angeloi, archangels, and archai

2. In our feelings we share in the life of the exusiai, dynamis and kyriotetes
3. In our will we share in the life of the seraphim, cherubim, and thrones

Our human lives, our destiny, is an affair or project of the gods. We need to learn to contemplate the destinies of human beings with reverence and awe.

Unit 21:
Sleep and Memory

Karmic Relationships, vol. 2, lectures 14 and 15

When we fall asleep, the physical and etheric are left in the bed. The astral and "I" go out through the head and the sense system. When we wake up again the astral and "I" approach us through the limbs, at first the tips of our fingers and toes and then the limbs and the rest of the body. The "I" likewise returns, enveloped by the astral body. It takes the whole day for the astral and "I" to fully arrive, right up to the head, only to start leaving again at night. Thus, the "I" and astral body are in constant flow, in movement. This has many implications for health and disease.

"It is precisely in the morning hours, when the astral body begins to rise upward from the limbs, that the unhealthy phenomena become manifest to a special faculty of perception. Therefore, in forming a judgement of illnesses it is of the utmost importance to know what feelings the patient has when he wakes from sleep, when his astral body is forcing upward what is unhealthy within him" (vol. 2, p. 218).

In the night, when the astral has passed out of the human being, karma begins to take shape, at first only in the form of pictures. What we have done throughout the day (good and bad) begins to be translated and integrated into the stream of karmic development (vol. 2, p.219).

As we continue to sleep, we start to dive down into the experiences from a preceding earthly life and then into the life before and so on until, by the time we wake again, we have reached and passed our very first life on Earth. (This happens even when we have short naps or fall asleep during a lecture!)

Thus, karma is perpetually present in our lives through sleep, inscribed as it were in the "world chronicle." And every time we fall asleep, we have an opportunity to approach our own karma. This is one of the greatest secrets of existence (see diagram from vol. 2, page 221).

a.) We look out into the world and pictures arise in our thoughts that represent what we perceive in the external world.

Unit 21: Sleep and Memory

b.) In a second situation, we live within a body, and thoughts well up containing the store of memories of what we have experienced in this present life on Earth.

See diagram (from vol. 2, p. 216): During earthly existence, we behold what it pleases the spirit beings to show us.

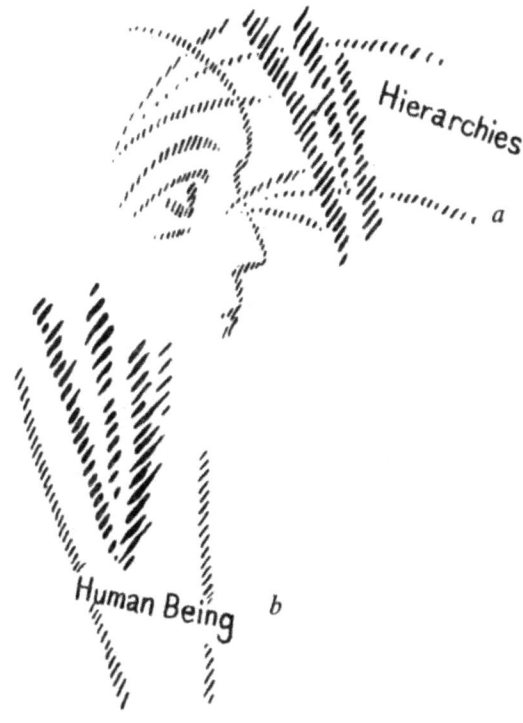

For example, two people can be born on the same street at the same time, grow up in the same town, go to the same school, and have similar experiences, yet if they go out to the park and look around, they will each see things differently. The world around us presents "sections" of itself and no two human beings see or experience things exactly the same way.

Consider memory: In everyday life we remember things we have experienced. In most cases, these memories come from within (see b in diagram). But we also have memory-thoughts that come to us from outside (see a in diagram)—these are not as dependent on us but come from the world around us. Two people can stand in the same park and will perceive very different things. How is this? **"During our earthly existence we behold what it pleases the spirit beings to reveal to us"** (vol. 2, p. 223). We take in not only what we open our eyes and ears to see and hear, but what the world and spirit beings wish to reveal to us! How is this possible? **"The hierarchies remember, just as human beings remember. What is it that provides the basis for the memory of the hierarchies? They look back upon our past earthly lives; that is what gives them the basis for their memory. According to what they behold in these past lives, they bring the appropriate section of the cosmos before our souls"** (vol. 2, p. 223).

We remember things in our present life through our self-generated memory, rising from within us. Memory thoughts come to us from without when we open ourselves up to the in-streaming of the cosmos.

The whole effort of the cosmos is intended so that the gods can bring knowledge of one's karma. Stars, clouds, sun, moon, plants, animals, stones, rivers, rocks, and mountains exist as a reservoir upon which the gods may draw **"to bring to our vision the primary form of our karma, according to the deeds we have wrought"** (vol. 2, p. 224). We are placed into the world so that we have an opportunity to discover the secrets of our existence.

Sleep and Midnight Sun as Seen by Initiates

Dawn to initiates is a cosmic remembrance of the vision of the Midnight Sun they beheld behind the Earth at midnight. In sleep the physical and etheric bodies are left in bed. All the thoughts we have had during the day leave traces in our physical and etheric body. We could not remember anything if this were not the case. "**All that we have thought during our waking life, from morning till evening, begins to move and ring on waves of sound.**... Beings who hover over us, rising and descending, busy themselves through our hours of sleep with the traces that have remained in our etheric bodies.... It is an immediate experience in them and absorbs their attention" (vol. 2, p. 234).

The third hierarchy (angels, archangels and archai) experiences these traces of thoughts living in our sleeping etheric body—all that lives as an echo of the day we have just completed. We create work for the angels during our time of sleep! Our thoughts are gathered by the angels at night and they then bear them out into the cosmos. This becomes part of the "record" inscribed in the cosmos, part of the universal "memory."

Unit 22:
Natural Disasters and Those Caused by Humans

Karmic Relationships, vol. 2, lecture 16

What are the karmic consequences of earthquakes, war, or accidents that occur with human inventions?

1. Railroad accidents (or today more likely cars, airplanes, etc.) are a result of human invention—usually only a few of the victims are karmically connected with one another.
2. With earthquakes and other natural disasters, many people are already bound together by common geographical location of birth, but as a result of the natural disaster they are torn out of their individual karma. Whether a death occurs in youth, middle age, or old age, the result is that their karma is "absolved." What does this mean? For the person who dies prematurely in this way (and does not experience the natural decline of etheric and physical that comes with ageing) something is brought into the spiritual world that would otherwise not have been there: an etheric, astral and "I"-organization—thus an earthly element streams into the spiritual world after a natural catastrophe. This brings ahrimanic powers to bear. How do the hierarchies respond to this? **"It then becomes the task of these spiritual beings to reintegrate into the world order what seems to have been turned to evil.... The gods have now to reckon with what confronts them in these circumstances so that they may transmute the ahrimanic evil into

a higher good" (vol. 2, p. 247). They then take hold of these under-utilized human forces and guide them in such a way as to strengthen the person inwardly for the next earthly incarnation. How? A nature-catastrophe evokes in human beings an intensified remembrance of what lies in their karma, and a strong intention develops to work constructively in the next life. These souls are more "karma-aware." In the case of a train accident or other events arising from the ingenuity of human invention, these accidents result in **oblivion concerning karma.** This oblivion makes for a more naïve, yet will-centered, next life. **"Whereas in the case of a natural catastrophe the intellectual qualities are intensified in the astral body of the victim, a catastrophe of civilization leads to a strengthening and enhancement of the will"** (vol. 2, p. 249).

3. Another possibility arises when people die owing to excessive emotionalism, group mind-set, nationalism, and so on, such as in war. Such emotions are often fanned by Lucifer, who helps flame wild passions and misguided instincts that, in many cases, are destructive. When people die in these circumstances, they bring these luciferic influences into the spiritual world with them. The gods thus have to contend with the in-streaming of both Lucifer and Ahriman. Thus, the destiny of the gods is interwoven with the destiny of human beings. They work to establish equilibrium. They seek to heal what comes through the portal of death from natural disasters, transportation accidents, and war—they seek to heal the influences of these three sources of destructive death. **"Beings of the Hierarchies hold us by the hand. And no one will be able to cultivate the right attitude toward knowledge of karma who does**

not perceive in karma the helping hand of the gods.... If I am to approach the holy ground of the spirit where something concerning karma can reveal itself to me, I must take the hand of the gods" (vol. 2, p. 253).

Unit 23:
The Universality of Thoughts

Karmic Relationships, vol. 3, lectures 1 and 2

Today we say, "I think," but in the past people lived with the sensation, "It thinks in me." Only feeling and willing were seen as personal, but thoughts were seen as coming from the ether that reaches up from Earth to the Moon. That is where thoughts lived, and just as people breathe in air, people then felt that, **"We perceive the thoughts, receive them into ourselves"** (vol. 3, p. 15). Thoughts were not a personal possession, but they existed and could be received. Thoughts are held during the time of our earthly life and then breathed out again—out into the cosmic spaces—when we pass through the gate of death. Thus, we share a common atmosphere of thought with all others who exist with us—we share a common atmosphere of thought that reaches out from Earth to the Moon (vol. 3, p. 16). **"The in-breathing of thoughts as the cosmic ether from the sublunary sphere—that is the beginning of life. The holding of the breath—that is earthly life itself. The out-breathing—that is the going forth of the thoughts once more, but with an individual human coloring, into the cosmic ether"** (vol. 3, p. 17).

In the three days after death, the human etheric body expands and thoughts spread out into the cosmos. After death, the thoughts received during earthly life live and weave in the cosmic ether that surrounds the Earth.

The preceding is a view of shared destiny. Others have wanted just to focus on the individuality of each separate human being. These two views form a spiritual contest.

Individual immortality (as the Dominicans portrayed) opposes universality and practices such as speaking to the dead. One impulse (individuality) has given us our consciousness soul, but the second also needs to be regained with a new inwardness of soul through spiritual-scientific knowledge.

These two streams live on even today: 1.) The universal life of thoughts that surrounds Earth, with inhaling and exhaling of soul and spirit; 2.) The independent life of each human being (with the benefit of freedom but also the danger of intellectualism and a contracted soul).

Animals are part of group-souls and have instincts. Humans also have instincts, but these come from former earth lives. Karma is our human instinct.

When we pass through the gate of death, we see our life spread out before us as a grand panorama. We see it all "from in front," while the vision of initiation sees it also from the other side, "from behind." People generally see things from only one side, but through initiation, when we are able to see it "from behind" as well, then we can see the whole web of karmic relationships. We see this web of karmic relationships arising from the thoughts that lived within the will during our earthly life. "**The thoughts we experience consciously during our earthly life are dead thoughts. But the thoughts that are woven into our karma, the thoughts that now emerge, are living. Thus, on 'the other side' of the life panorama, as it were, living thoughts spring forth. And now (this is a fact of untold significance) the beings of the third hierarchy draw near and receive what is springing forth from the 'other side'** of the panorama. Angels, archangels and archai draw it into themselves; they breathe it in!" (vol. 3, p. 31).

In this process the freed etheric of the individual (which continues after death) brings life to the thoughts and gives them to the third hierarchy. "**Archangels and archai in the weaving ether receive the human being's web of destiny**" (vol. 3, p. 32).

> **Assignment:** Try using the preceding quotation as a meditation. My thoughts are received by the hierarchies.

Then, when the etheric body is dissolved and the thoughts have all been breathed in by the angels, archangels and archai, after a few days one enters the backward review of the previous life, whereby one experiences past deeds, tendencies of thought, will impulses, and so on from the perspective of how they affected other people. One goes right into the minds and feelings of others. We experience **"all that took place in the depths of other human beings' souls with whom we had any kind of relationship—to whom we did anything whatever, good or ill. And once again it shows itself, how what human beings thus experience is received...the consequences of our actions, transformed in righteousness and justice, are taken up into the exusiai, dynamis, and kyriotetes"** (vol. 3, p. 34).

For meditation: **"In exusiai, dynamis, and kyriotetes, in the astral feeling of the cosmos, the righteous consequences of our earthly life die into the realm of being"** (vol. 3, p. 35). By seeing "the other side" of the pictures of earthly life we are able to "die into" the cosmos. The German word *verwesen* means fading, dying, a destructive process, passing out of existence, and having as its core meaning "to carry the real being away," or in today's language, to forgive, forego, or give away.

> **Assignment:** Discuss this in groups or with another person.

Then the third phase after death occurs whereby a person journeys even further, right back to the starting point of the previous earthly life. Now we enter through Sun forces into the essential spirit land, where the earthly deeds, now transformed into the Divine Righteousness, are received by the first hierarchy: **"In thrones and cherubim and seraphim, as their deeds of being, our justly transmuted 'fruits of the earthly life' are resurrected"** (vol. 3, p. 35).

All three stages then work into our next life, manifesting as an "instinct for karma."

Unit 24:
Our Connection to the Stars

Karmic Relationships, vol. 3, lecture 3

Every person has a personal star that determines what has been gathered between death and a new birth. We each come from the direction of a certain star. When we look up at night and see all the stars, we can have a fullness of heart and mind, for the twinkling stars reflect all of humanity, and we feel united with the cosmos.

When we are born, the Sun is in a specific relationship to each person's particular star. Then every year, when we have a birthday, that configuration returns, but with a slight alteration—the Sun is slightly behind the same time and place of the previous year, until at age seventy-two, when the Sun has remained behind for a whole cosmic day. **"After that time, the Sun can no longer comfort the star, which it could comfort while it stood before it and covered it. The star has become free again for the soul-spiritual work of the human being within the cosmos"** (vol. 3, p. 46). We can experience this wisdom of the Sun and stars with reverence and know that whatever happens here on Earth has a connection, a particular correspondence in the spiritual world.

As for individual karma, **"what is unconscious in one life becomes a degree more conscious in the next life on Earth"** (vol. 3, p. 50). For those working with Anthroposophy, the question of karma often arises in a "more intensive way," which can bring both rewards and challenges in karmic studies. While it can be more poignant or gripping, it is not necessarily easier to comprehend. For instance, a musician who attends a concert might have a more minutely technical understanding of the performance, but does not necessarily enjoy it or feel it more deeply in the soul than someone who lacks the musical expertise or background.

When someone experiences shame, it can easily morph into hatred. Through our work with karma, we can make ourselves a stronger vessel for destiny.

> **Assignment:** Discuss foregoing ideas, letting go of habitual thoughts.

UNIT 25:
KARMIC RELATIONSHIPS AND ISSUES
OF THE 21ST CENTURY

Karmic Relationships, vol. 3, lectures 5 and 6

Before the fourteenth century, human beings had a rich dream life and a strong intermediate feeling sensation between sleeping and waking that was delicate, light, and intimate. This happened because the "I" did not immediately absorb the astral body; rather, it remained through the night and into the early stages of waking. Thus, this feeling arose: **"I have been living in a world filled with light, one in which all manner of things were happening"** (vol. 3, p. 73). Pictures of something that had taken place in sleep remained after waking.

When people of that time looked out upon the world of plants, they saw the meadowland as though there was a slight and gentle bluish-red cloud, or halo, spread over it, **"especially at the time of day when the Sun was shining less brightly (past the height of noontime), as though a bluish-red light, like a luminous mist with manifold and moving waves and colors, were spread over the flowering meadow"** (vol. 3, p. 73).

When people looked at animals, they saw not only the physical shapes, but also how they were enveloped in an astral aura: **"Slightly, delicately, and intimately, this aura was seen ... when the Sunlight was working in a rather gentle way"** (vol. 3, p. 74). Everywhere in outer nature, people still perceived the spiritual working and weaving.

> **Assignment:** What are the implications for environmental consciousness through the ideas just described? Indigenous cultures had such awareness. The loss of cultures and nature consciousness went hand in hand. Environmental and social justice are closely connected.

After passing into death, human beings had a recollection of this nature consciousness and a sense that the Father-God was speaking. After the etheric body was laid aside a few days after death, the human being lived in the astral body and had a feeling: in my astral body now after death, I am experiencing all that I thought and did on Earth. In the astral, in which I lived during sleep, I now (after death) have a much clearer feeling than the vague feelings experienced while on Earth. **"Now, in the time between death and a new birth, as in his astral body he returned through his past earthly life, he had the feeling: 'Behold, in this my astral body lives the Christ. I just did not notice it. In reality, however, my astral body dwelled in the essence and being of Christ every night'"** (vol. 3, p. 75). Thus, they knew that, for *as long as we go backward through our earthly life after death, Christ would not desert us, for Christ was always present in the astral body*. Christ is in the astral and the Father God is in the etheric and in all of the natural world.

In ancient times, people did not speak of abstract laws of nature but about the Goddess Natura, who worked creatively in all outer nature. The goddess Persephone/Proserpina (Greek/Roman) appeared in every mineral, plant, beast, cloud, and mountain, and changed with the seasons. The planetary system revealed knowledge of the human soul: **"Learn how the wandering stars hold sway in the heavens, and you will**

know how your own soul works and weaves and lives within you" (vol. 3, p. 89). This was placed before the students of the esoteric schools so that they could approach the Great Ocean that leads from the planets, the wandering stars, to the fixed stars—thus one could learn the secrets of the "I" by learning secrets of the universe. [Note to reader: At this point Steiner begins a description of the School of Chartres, with its two streams and its relation to the anthroposophic movement. We need to recognize the language of the Spirit of Time, the Zeitgeist.]

> **Assignment:** What is the language of the spirit of our time? Can we learn to read the intentions of our time?

UNIT 26:
INTELLIGENCE

Karmic Relationships, vol. 3, lectures 7–9

Freedom, through a greater use of human intelligence, is a gift of the years leading up to the end of the nineteenth century. Now, in the twenty-first century, we need to reconnect with the spiritual worlds, yet old habits of thinking remain from the Gabriel age. These were strongly rooted in the forces of heredity when humans felt their qualities were dependent on heredity—aspects inherited from his ancestors.

It is a central task of our time to properly appreciate the heritage of our ancestors while not being totally bound by bloodlines and heredity. "**This Intelligence, formally cosmic, had become earthly. And there was Ahriman, wanting to make it altogether earthly. He wants to make it continue in the way that began during the age of Gabriel, making it earthly—an affair only of human communities of blood, an affair of generations and the forces of reproduction and inheritance. Ahriman desires all of this**" (vol. 3, p. 112).

"**True anthroposophists must be *conscious*, for the need today is to look with active participation and to cooperate in the battle between Ahriman and Michael**" (vol. 3, p. 117).

Discouragement is everywhere! Those who worked in the ancient mystery centers of Greece, Egypt, Ephesus, and elsewhere have been discouraged by the spread of the illusion of materialism all over the world. Our time is one of trial and probation. Even the teachings of Plato have become "**a kind of watery extract of the ancient mysteries**" (vol. 3, p. 125). Why? The strength of Ahriman has increased. We can imagine him with a receding forehead, a cynical expression, lower forces ruling intelligence—an intelligence that has become *personal intelligence*, logical, scornful, and contemptuous in thought. Michael's intelligence, however, is "**something belonging to all humankind—the common and universal intelligence that benefits all human beings alike**" (vol. 3, p. 127).

> Assignment: What are the implications of the two forms of intelligence for social life, and modern environmental, economic, and social justice?

Raphael is the spirit connected most frequently to the art of healing, but "**it is Michael who brings human karma nearest of all to health and to disease**" (vol. 3, p. 135). Michael works not only in a cosmopolitan sense, but also helps to tear us away from the narrower earthly connections of life and lift us to spiritual heights, and this influences the karma of those who belong to the stream of Michael. At the same time, those who work with Michael feel things more deeply and incisively than those who might have remained indifferent.

When a person's consciousness is lowered and a person is overcome by faintness, ahrimanic forces become more effective. Michael needs the luciferic spirits; he needs their cooperation as a polar antithesis to Ahriman. Human beings of Michael are placed in the midst of the battle, the interplay between the two impulses of Lucifer and Ahriman.

> Assignment: Study *The Representative of Humanity* statue, located at the Goetheanum in Dornach.

Karmic Reconciliation

The Representative of Humanity, *Rudolf Steiner's 24-foot-high carving*

We are living in a time of great decisions. How do anthroposophists and those who are not anthroposophists relate to each other? Anthroposophists work to dissolve old karma. For those who remain outside this work, new karma is woven. When the two stand in relationship to each other, a decision must be made!

> **Assignment:** How do members and friends of the Anthroposophical Society relate to non-members? Internally, we are resolving old karma, but externally we have choices in weaving new karma. What are the implications?

Today people identify as French, Turkish, English, and so on. But those who today "receive Anthroposophy with inner force of soul, with deep impulse and strength of heart—who receive it, therefore, as the deepest force of their life—such distinctions will lack meaning when they return to Earth next. People will ask: Where do they come from? They do not belong to any nation; they do not claim any race—it is as though they have grown away from all races and nations" (vol. 3, p. 140).

Michael's influence is to use Cosmic Intelligence and penetrate the earthly element, transforming differences so that one no longer seems to belong to only one country—this is a physically creative, formative power. This also makes it more difficult for anthroposophists in the next generation to come to terms with the world as it is. "In this situation, as an anthroposophist, one's karma will be more difficult to experience than it is for others.... To be true anthroposophists, we must be able to observe our own experience of karma with constant wide-awake attention. If we do not, then our comfortable, easy-going experiencing of karma—or, rather, our desire to experience it so—will find expression and take vengeance in physical illnesses, physical accidents, and the like" (vol. 3, p. 141).

There is also a division in the angelic realm: angels who accompany anthroposophists in the next incarnation will be able to rise more fully into the spiritual kingdoms, whereas angels who accompany non-anthroposophists will descend. Thus, a twofold kingdom of angeloi is being created by the way we are on the Earth.

Unit 27:
Karmic Restoration

Karmic Relationships, vol. 3, lectures 10 and 11

When we educate children in Waldorf schools, they have such a wide view of humanity and see such wide horizons that they see many, many possibilities for life going forward and can imagine all sorts of future pathways (p. 149). Those who work with anthroposophy need to be people of initiative. We cannot escape two big influences in the modern world: intellectualism and materialism. We cannot withdraw from interacting with our world, **"but we *must* be contemporaries of our age—that is to say, we must have a feeling of what is going on in our own time"** (vol. 3, p. 152). Some anthroposophists prefer to "paddle in the Timeless"—they are like the bee that is afraid to use the sting of initiative, of stinging into the Ahrimanic realm **"through an undetermined fear of life the initiative remains inactive"** (vol. 3, p. 153). Materialism is not wrong, it is quite right, but only in the physical realm; **"materialism is right *in its own domain*"** (vol. 3, p. 154).

"In that future time, the karmic affinities, karmic relationships, will make themselves felt far less. But of all the karmic relationships this will have remained: those who are standing in the field of materialism will have to see and witness those who stand in the field of spirituality…will see with their own eyes and touch with their hands those with whom they were once karmically united, perceiving in their physiognomy, in their whole expression, what the spirit really is, for it will have become creative in outer form and feature. In such human beings it will thus be proved, visibly for human eyes, what the spirit is as a creative power in the world...what spirit truly *is*" (vol. 3, p. 157).

"Angels are the beings who guide people from earthly life to earthly life. They are the beings next above us along our path in the life between death and a new birth, showing us the way for our return to earthly life. They make our several earthly lives into a connected chain, a totality of human life" (p. 167).

> **Assignment:** What does it mean to connect with your angel—find your spirit guide?

"The angel of the one human being—the one human soul who was karmically connected with another human soul—did not go on with the angel of that other soul. Of two human souls karmically connected to each another, one angel remained with Michael while the other descended to Earth.... [Thus] the karma of human beings became disordered. This is to pronounce one of the deepest and most important words that can possibly be spoken with regard to the modern history of humankind. Disorder entered the karma of present-day humanity. In the following lives on Earth, human experiences were no longer all properly coordinated with their karma. This is the chaotic element in recent history. This has brought into the history of recent times increasing social chaos—chaos of civilization. And the disorder that has entered human karma can find no end. A split has occurred in the hierarchy of angeloi belonging to Michael" (vol. 3, pp. 171–72).

"Michael himself is bringing the power which is to *bring order again into karma* of those who have gone with him....

Unit 27: Karmic Restoration

Members of the Anthroposophical Society...are to bring order again into their karma.... It is *the restoration of the truth in karma* (vol. 3, p. 173).

The task before us is karmic restoration.

See comments on Friedrich Nietzsche and Ahriman (vol. 3, pp. 175–76).

Unit 28:
Sacredness of Place

Karmic Relationships, vol. 4, lectures 1 and 2

Preparatory assignments: We already recognize that our karma is resting in lower levels of consciousness. Now we need to bring it into consciousness:

1. Use indigenous materials and environmentalism to work with the foregoing thoughts.
2. Do a comparative study of trees to help us experience their intrinsic character;
3. Use geography to influence memory and recollect past experiences. Karmic memory felt in one's back space, behind the head, is diffused and vague. Biographical memory is heart-centered and piercing, charging one's breathing when present.

There are three states of human consciousness in the context of evolution: waking, dreaming, sleeping (vol. 4, p 20). In primeval times, humans were in a condition of evening twilight. Now we have a "morning dawn" consciousness that can arise by strengthening our soul forces, so we **"learn to look at every tree or rock, every spring or mountain, or at the stars in such a way that the spiritual fact or spiritual being behind every physical thing is revealed"** (vol. 4, p. 22).

Meditation: look at a tree. Even though it is a physical reality, let it become a void, leaving a space for the gaze and for the spirit being of the tree to meet oneself. **"As the physical light is reflected back to our physical eyes, so the divine-spiritual, all-pervading essence of the Sun can be reflected back as a reality to our eyes of the soul from every earthly being" (vol. 4, p. 23). We see not just that "the rose is red" but how it is giving back to us the gift of the physical-etheric Sun nature, the Sun that streams through the world with all-quickening life. *And when we develop the forces of the soul, we can penetrate with our vision into the life of dreamless sleep; we can discover the connections of karma.*

> **Assignment:** Reflect on your biographical geographic memories: 1.) Have you returned for a visit to a place where you once lived? How did it affect you? 2.) Have you ever gone to a place you have never seen before in this life and felt a connection?

There is a sacredness of place. Geography speaks to us of past experiences—this is part of the ancient tradition of visiting an oracle or a sacred place on Earth.

Unit 29:
Looking for Karmic Connections

Karmic Relationships, vol. 4, lectures 2 and 3

"A human life, after all, appears in its true nature only when we consider how it passes through repeated lives on Earth.... For when we investigate these things in reality, we find that the continued thread of karma or destiny goes far deeper into the inner being of a human being and is little connected with a person's outer profession or inner calling. It is far more concerned with the inner forces of soul and soul resistances, with moral relationships that can, after all, reveal themselves in any and every calling.... The investigation of karma—the thread of destiny—requires us to concentrate on circumstances in a human life that may often appear outwardly trivial or of little importance" (vol. 4, pp. 26–27).

In one example of reincarnation, Steiner observed a person who habitually used his handkerchief to blow his nose just before giving a lecture! Then Steiner often saw this person with another man, and something about the pair intrigued him. He discovered that many lives earlier this lecturer had been embalmed in ancient Egypt as a mummy (which still existed). He had been a chieftain in Egypt, even attained an initiation, but over time he had become decadent. This man had a servant, and together their task was to embalm mummies, a very complicated process. As the chieftain became increasingly frivolous in regard to his duties, more responsibility fell on the servant, who eventually became an expert. Thanks to the knowledge needed for embalming, this servant became quasi-initiated. After they died, they returned to Earth. The chieftain (who had experienced a bitterness as a result of his former life) came back as Julia, the daughter of Augustus, and she eventually married Tiberius, the step-son of Augustus. Both led an immoral life and were banished.

The other man, the former servant, came back as Titus Livius, or Livy, the famous historian of Roman history. Some of the very people he had mummified returned as some of the seven Roman kings, which Livy then wrote about in his books as a historian. His knowledge of human nature gained from mummification manifested as deep insight into the Roman rulers and as light, readable prose. Then, after death and another journey in the spiritual world, Livy came back as the poet, Walter von der Vogelweide, in Tyrol (Italian Alps), where he discovered the Castle of the Rocks, the home of the Dwarf King Laurin (who had been the former Chieftain in Egypt.) This person was an alchemist and a former chieftain.

This leads us to a karmic law: **"We see the same individuals drawn together again and again, called to Earth simultaneously, complementing one another, and living in a kind of mutual contrast"** (vol. 4, p. 35). But capacities are transformed—embalming mummies changed into poetry and a celebration of life's fullness. Then, for his next incarnation he returned as Ludwig Schleich (1859–1922), a medical doctor during Rudolf Steiner's time. And the former chieftain came back again as August Strindberg. One can read in the memoirs of Ludwig Schleich his relationship to Strindberg (1849–1912). These were the two men Steiner had observed together at his lectures.

Chieftain who performed mummification in Egypt—
   Julia, wife of Tiberius—King Laurin—August Strindberg
Servant—Livy—Walter von der Vogelweide—Ludwig Schleich

We live in connection with other individuals over many lifetimes.

Another example is Haroun al Raschid, a ruler in Asia Minor, who gathered the most eminent spiritual and intellectual figures of his time at his court. Architecture, poetry, astrology, geography, history, and anthropology were all brilliantly represented. Some of those people even carried within them much of the knowledge of ancient initiation sciences. Raschid was able to bring together the arts and sciences in his court advisors, which became a great academy of the East. The most significant contributor was his "counselor," who possessed extraordinary insights and provided the greatest service to Haroun al Raschid. When these two individuals died, they spent a long time together in the spiritual worlds.

Another earthly schooling path was represented by Aristotle and Alexander the Great. At the Fourth Council of Constantinople in 869, the trichotomy of body, soul, and spirit was declared heretical. It was decreed that the church could teach that humans have only a body and soul. This had tremendous significance (see vol. 4, pp. 46–50; the responses included the Order of King Arthur and Tintagel).

Haroun al Raschid carried his Arabic wisdom into the spiritual world and then reincarnated with this knowledge, but in a new form appropriate for a new age. He returned as Francis Bacon. Influenced more by Christianity in its evolving form, his wise counselor returned as Amos Comenius. Both were spiritually influenced by and responded to the Council of 869.

Some of those connected with the Aristotelian stream came back as members of the School of Chartres. "It is interesting to see the manifold ways in which that spiritual life radiated out. In France, in one place after another, we can see how, even in the teachings that were given, the spirit of Chartres lived on in the high schools carried over into Southern France, even into Italy. But it lived not only in the teachings; it also lived on in an immediately spiritual way. It is interesting how Brunetto Latini, having been an ambassador in Spain during a certain time, returned to Florence, the city of his fathers, heard of its misfortune even from a distance, and thus suffered a powerful convulsion of his soul, to which was added a slight attack of sunstroke. In this bodily condition, a human being is easily accessible to spiritual influences that work in a spiritual way. It is indeed well known how Brunetto Latini, on his way to Florence, experienced what was actually a kind of elementary initiation. Brunetto Latini became Dante's teacher, and the spirituality of the *Comedia* proceeds from the teachings that Latini gave to his pupil Dante" (vol. 4, p. 54).

> **Assignment:** If interested, research these key figures:
>
> Haroun al Raschid and John Amos Comenius
> Brunetto Latini and Dante
> Aristotle and Alain de Lille

Unit 30:
Images of the School of Chartres

Karmic Relationships, vol. 4, lectures 4 and 5

Following a review of the Aristotelian and Platonic streams, investigate more on School of Chartres, Latini, Cistercians, and Rudolf Steiner's connection to them:

There is a link with indigenous cultures: "...those who thus looked into the life and movement of the elements—earth, water, air, and fire—did not see more natural laws, but behind all this life and movement they saw a great and living being, the Goddess Natura...what we cannot see, what is hidden from us in the darkness of sleep, works in all the activities of the elements, in wind and weather, in all that surrounds us and constitutes us," (vol. 4, p. 59). So, too, with Persephone, the Goddess who ascends for half of the time, "revealing herself in the outer movement and activity of physical sense, nature, and who, on the other hand, descends nightly and yearly to live and work in fields of creation, hidden from human beings by the dark consciousness of sleep" (vol. 4, p. 59).

People of the Middle Ages also looked up to the zodiac, the planets and the constellations, to see the spiritual powers living in the starry heavens. Humans were seen as the microcosm of the greater macrocosm.

A monk in the School of Chartres who was especially devoted to its teachings reincarnated as Elisabeth Gluck (1814–1894). She adopted Betty Paoli as her pen name as a writer and poet. It seemed that she often longed to die and had no connection to her time on Earth. This mood of soul came from her continuing connection to her time at Chartres and **"the evening twilight mood of a living Platonism"** (vol. 4, p. 75). What is most unusual in this case of reincarnation was a physical likeness in two lives: "**...the faces of yonder monk and the author of the present time were indeed extraordinarily alike**" (vol. 4, p. 76).

There are two kinds of souls in the anthroposophic movement:

1. Those who had deep connection to and understanding of Christianity in former lives;
2. Those who in previous lives had a strong connection to the ancient "heathen" mysteries.

Although there is often a physical starting point, karma is most helpful in tracing the spiritual life of a person in the inner life of soul.

Unit 31:
Karmic Timing

Karmic Relationships, vol. 4, lectures 4–6

Each of the organs in our body points us in the direction of the universe. They are the microcosm of the macrocosm. "For the sum-total of the human organs...leads to perceptions that correspond in turn to the spiritual perception of the former human earthly lives...in reality, the whole past of human beings lives in the present" (vol. 4, p. 81).

> **Assignment:** Review the organs as outlined in *Organizational Integrity* by TF and how they relate to cosmic forces and the planets.

Parsifal: "Julian the Apostate could speak of the threefold Sun and many cosmic truths. He rejected Christianity because of misrepresentations.... And he was consequently murdered. He was seen as a betrayer of the mysteries, but the murder was prearranged" (vol. 4, p. 82). If conditions had been more favorable at the time, Julian could have brought about an understanding of how the ancient mysteries were a continuation from the pre-Christian Christ, the Logos, leading right up to the Mystery of Golgotha. But he was murdered and prevented from presenting these connections.

In his next life, he returned in the Middle Ages as Herzeleide, the mother of Parsifal. She married Gamuret, who lost his life in treachery during the eastern campaign, but through her anguish she came to understand her destiny: Herzeleide, the woman who prepared and then sent her son Parsifal out to seek and find the esoteric paths for Christianity. The soul is affected by experiences in each life on Earth; it changes and transforms. "Life as Herzeleide spread itself over the former life as Julian the Apostate, like a warm embalming cloud. Thus, the soul grew more intense, deeper, and inner, growing richer, as well, in manifold impulses of the inner life" (vol. 4, p. 85). All of this helped Tycho Brahe bring new perception and depth to astronomy, despite having only limited instruments to work with. Brahe also helped other souls prepare to incarnate—especially Platonists. Many of them had been waiting to incarnate again at the end of the twentieth century (see vol. 4, page 90), to return to Earth as anthroposophists.

"Those who receive Anthroposophy in a sincere way at the present time are preparing their souls to shorten, insofar as possible, the life between death and a new birth, and to appear again at the end of the twentieth century, united with the teachers of Chartres, who remained behind" (vol. 4, p. 99).

Unit 32:
Karmic Balance

Karmic Relationships, vol. 4, lectures 7–9

After dying, we live with intense reality through the experiences we had in the *nights* of our life on Earth—about a third of our time on Earth in the previous life. We live through it backwards. We see all that we went through from the viewpoint of others, the people who met us. If we hurt someone, we feel what they felt when that happened. This journey after death through the lens of the other creates in us a great desire for karmic balance in the next life.

For when we are in the spiritual world (after death) we go through a Moon phase where we meet the great "Registrars" of our destiny, the teachers of humanity who help us learn the lessons needed. Some of their traditions are contained in the sacred literature of various cultures.

> **Assignment:** Which sacred texts and sources have you found to be the most helpful in your life thus far? Why?

From an opposite perspective, **"we can study karma of the cleverest men of the present day—cleverest in the materialistic sense—and we find that as a rule in former earthly lives they had something to do with cosmological aberrations into the realms of black magic"** (vol. 4, p. 112). By contrast, many peasants and country folk have often had an aversion to people who are far too clever. Those who are connected to nature and the land are in tune with the etheric and the innate wisdom of the universe, as was the case for indigenous people, and they do not value cleverness as a virtue (especially the manipulative kind).

When we look at successive lives of people as in our karma study, we are also going to learn more about the course of history in general. For example, Agrippa—a Greek sceptic and first-century cynic—joked about the most important matters of his time. Christianity and spirituality passed him by. He took mischievous delight in trivializing things. When he journeyed after death and entered the Moon region of "wise teachers," he was encouraged to look back at his former life when pagan rituals still ruled but Christianity was expected. He was, so to speak, prepared to deal with cults and rituals.

In his next life, he incarnated as Cardinal Mazarin (1602–1661), a high official who advised Louis XIV and even ran the government when King Louis was a child. He now ruled over European religion with the style he had learned in Asia Minor. He was a great statesman with a wide sweep of vision, yet he became intoxicated by his own deeds (though they did not arise from the depths of his heart).

Then in his next incarnation he was reborn as Georg von Hertling (1843–1919), Chancellor of Germany, who actually did rule, but with a kind of religious fervor.

As another example, there was a man who had failed to influence the Council of Nicaea who later withdrew as a hermit to contemplate the origin of inspiration in thought. He was born again during the Middle Ages as a visionary woman who had wonderful insight into the spiritual world. She gave herself up mystically to Christ. She had visions in which he appeared to her as the leader of peaceful hosts who brought peace to the world through gentleness. This nun had remarkable visions. Then, in the next life, this individual incarnated in Russia as the mystic and author Vladimir Solovyov (1853–1900), who brought so much depth and meaning to his work.

The next succession of Earth lives demonstrates how hindrances arise that prevent the carrying of spiritual content from one life into another: A Jewish woman of the late sixth century escaped from Babylonian captivity to Asia Minor, where, thanks to a special teacher, she was able to study Zoroastrianism and the dualism of light and dark. This opportunity awakened her as a seer, allowing visions of the cosmic order. As a result, she was able to behold a rich tableau of Imaginations.

After the journey after death, she (as well as her teacher) was reborn in the late fifth century as a man. In this life, he was influenced by Martianus Capella, father of the well-known Seven Liberal Arts (rhetoric, grammar, logic, music, arithmetic, geometry, and astronomy), each of which was seen as a living being. He learned to speak the "language" of these liberal arts and was inspired by them. He again came into close contact with his teacher from his past life, who was now on Earth as a woman of great intelligence. But the man in this life brought his visionary life from his feminine incarnation to bear on his connection to the cosmic laws in reproduction and creation.

After another journey through death, these two were born again, this time both as men. The woman who was originally a Jewish refugee now became, in the third incarnation, the Italian Utopian Thomaso Campanella (1568–1639; see descriptions in vol. 4, pp. 132–33). He fought for the liberation of southern Italy and was taken prisoner by the Spaniards.

He was held in Cosenza Prison for twenty-seven years. While in prison he became friends with a Jewish cabalist—the same teacher and friend from earlier incarnations.

While in prison, he worked on a utopian picture of a future society: "**In his work on a Solar State, he conceives and describes a social Utopia wherein he imagines that, by a rational configuration of the social life, everyone may become happy**" (vol. 4, p. 134). All would be administered according to astrological principles, even marriage and conception. He believed in the power of the Sun to bring down cosmic wisdom to order society—all imagined while in prison for so many years, able only to peer through narrow slits at the sunshine of nature—whereas, in his soul, all sorts of emotional experiences from past lives tormented him. Finally, he was freed from prison by Pope Urban. He went to Paris, found favor with Richelieu, and received a pension that sustained him for his remaining years.

Campanella died and went through the journey of death and returned as someone who became highly intellectual, with a great urge to repudiate his former spiritual life. He came back in a "childlike body," a boy, precocious with the maturity of someone in his thirties—thus, in a way, trying to make up for the lost decades when he was previously imprisoned. Although not required in school, he forced himself to learn Spanish, thus confronting the episode of his Spanish imprisonment—again the work of karma. The bitterest thing for him while imprisoned now enters the subconscious region through learning Spanish. When older, this person, known to us as Otto Weininger (1880–1903), studied philosophy at the University of Vienna and earned a PhD. He wrote his dissertation, titled *Sex and Character,* focusing on gender in a way that some of his ancient primeval concepts from past lives played through, though looking at Nature: "The light that shines forth in nature is the manifestation of morality. One who knows light knows true morality. Hence, in the deep-sea fauna and flora that lives without the light, we must seek the source of all immorality on Earth" (vol. 4, p. 139). He overcame some of the hatred of his last lives (exile as a woman, imprisonment as a man) to show how light transforms evil to good. One strange habit he acquired toward the end of his life was looking out at the light through narrow slits he made in a darkened room. He loved doing this—another echo of his past life as a prisoner. But he could not bear to see the sunset. He also had epilepsy, which Steiner attributed to a kind of repetition of his former imprisonment—"his attacks were acts of repulsion and defiance" (vol. 4, p. 140).

At one point he suddenly hurried off to Italy, then returned to the mountains near Vienna. He took a room in the house where Beethoven died until he finished his writing and lived through the effects of imprisonment. He then shot himself. Why? He had the idea that if he continued living, he would have become a thoroughly bad man.

Steiner: "Look at the world of Otto Weininger, my dear friends. You will see all the hindrances in a soul who is placed so abnormally...hindrances that stand in the way and prevent finding the spiritual...how many hindrances there are in the Age of Michael to hinder a person from doing full justice to this Age" (vol. 4, p. 141). "If he had been able to acquire a spiritual worldview, he could have continued in his evolution" (vol. 4, p. 141).

Unit 32: Karmic Balance

Assignment: What is the task of anthroposophy in a world of hindrances? What is the "karma" of suicide?

Unit 33:
Plato

Karmic Relationships, vol. 4, lecture 10

The roles of Intellectualism and spirituality weave together through Plato's influence. For Plato, "Ideas" were active genii, attainable in imaginative vision—vivid images, shades of being. But gradually, over the course of history, these living ideas were taken by people in an increasingly abstract and shadowy way. **"In Plato everything is alive, and in Plato above all this perception is alive: that the Ideas are the foundations of all things present in the world of sense. Where we turn our gaze in the world of sense, what we behold, it is the outward expression and manifestation of Ideas"** (vol. 4, p. 147).

Platonic Love is thoroughly spiritual and has set aside, insofar as possible, the egoism frequently mingled with love— **"this spiritualized devotion to the world, to life, to humans, to God, to the Idea, thoroughly permeates the Platonic view of life"** (vol. 4, p. 148). He was Christian in a pre-Christian time if, by *Christianity,* we mean the love of a Sun being.

There was a young artist who came under Plato's influence—not a disciple but a follower. Plato noticed him and perceived in him infinite promise. Then, several incarnations later this young artist incarnated as Goethe, carrying this Platonic influence into his next significant earthly life.

Plato himself however found "the greatest difficulty in entering a new incarnation," and it took him a long time—he resisted entering a heavily Roman/Christian time period in

Europe. He needed "a bodily organism into which he might carry his former impulses in a way that they might now come forth again with a Christian coloring" (vol. 4, p. 149). Plato was so Greek that he had an aversion to returning as a Roman.

Finally, he returned in the tenth century as the nun Hrotsvitha (935–973), a remarkable person who could write dramas and bring the whole culture of the time as an **"astonishing personality"** (vol. 4, p. 152). After death, the spirit of Plato and Hrotsvitha wrestled with each other and, in the next incarnation, returned to Earth as Karl Julius Schröer (1825–1900), a teacher and friend of Rudolf Steiner. Schröer was fascinated by many aspects of Goethe and wrote a book on Goethe and love—the paternal, Plato–artist connection of earlier incarnations was now reciprocated in Schröer. He told Steiner he wanted to write a biography of Goethe, but never did—he said Goethe was **"continually visiting my soul"** (vol. 4, p. 155)

The incarnations—Plato, Hrotsvitha, and the influences of a young artist and Goethe all came together in the soul of Karl Julius Schröer and heavily influenced Rudolf Steiner.

Schröer embodied the question: *"How shall we bring spirituality into the life of the present time?"* (vol. 4, p. 157).

Unit 34:
Human Connections

Karmic Relationships, vol. 5, lectures 1 and 2

There are two types of meetings. The first is when we feel an immediate connection, regardless of outer appearances or circumstances. It is an inward sense of being connected, and we don't want to talk about the person. The second makes an intellectual impression upon us, and may be with a person whom we might not feel personally connected to. To talk about this person is easy, and we can describe this person physically and precisely, but without an inner affinity.

> **Assignment**: List people with whom you quickly realized there was an inner connection. Then list a few examples of people you have worked with who might have impressed you for some reason or other, but with whom there is little inner connection.

A historical case of instantaneous connection occurred to Giuseppe Garibaldi. He was on a voyage off the coast of Brazil, and through a telescope saw a girl standing on the shore. He immediately knew she would become his partner. When he landed, a man greeted him at the dock and invited Garibaldi to dinner. That night he discovered that the man was the father of the girl he had seen through the telescope, Anita Ribeiro. Even before the meal was served, Garibaldi proposed. He spoke only Italian and she only Portuguese, yet she understood his proposal and accepted. They had a beautiful relationship. This is an example of a karmic connection. She, too, was heroic and accompanied him on his military campaigns in South America. She cared for him when he was wounded and bore a child with him, whom she strapped around her neck during military campaigns. This relationship helped Garibaldi find a firmer foothold in life. When she died some years later, Garibaldi remarried in a completely "conventional way."

"When we study karmic experiences like that of an acquaintanceship—where beauty or ugliness counts for nothing but where the feeling of kinship wells up entirely from within—we are led to discern the influence of those beings of whom I have said that they were the original, primal teachers of humankind; they have remained active to this day, but now they work from outside, from the cosmos. Such relationships are of special interest to these Moon beings and through them they participate in the most intimate way in the evolution of earthly humanity.

"Just as there are beings who belong to the Moon, so there are beings who belong to the Sun. We have spoken of relationships in which we find it easy to describe the other person in a more external way. In these cases, it is the *Sun beings* who interest themselves in the threads that are woven between soul and soul" (vol. 5, p. 17).

Consider these two types of connection:

1. Will—we meet someone who stirs something within us. A past life connection is likely.
2. External meeting—we observe, receive impressions, and hear ideas. We are meeting for the first time in the present.

The Moon beings, Moon "books," make it possible to read in their records *before* we descend to Earth. Some old portraits from ancient times show a human figure, and behind it and a little higher is a second, and behind that is a third figure. Thus, an initiate sees previous incarnations in a person in the present.

We experience people we have known before this life as when we are in a dark, mysterious night, and then when we get to know them the bright light of day seems to take the place of the mysterious night. This is what happens between two people who are karmically connected. Moon beings weave into our astral body the karma that is past. It is mutual; both persons may experience this with each other.

When we meet people whom we have not known before for the first time in this life, there are now shadowy pictures of earthly lives behind them. Instead, an initiate sees beings of the next higher hierarchies appear in the background along with rays of the Sun. These Sun beings weave into our "I"-organization what is to take place after our first meeting with this other person on Earth, the basis of our *future* karma. The present is always changing into the future. You feel the angels and archangels standing behind the person.

> **Discussion**: Have you experienced Moon versus Sun relationships, and if so, how was that? Share examples.

Moon beings are connected with a person's past, yet the past is continuously still working in us when we feel impelled toward another person who draws us inwardly. When an initiate meets another person, a whole series of pictures well up, like a script one can read. We recognize the human being standing physically before us, thanks to the picture of experiences shared in common in earlier Earth lives. All in the Akasha substance as living reality, thanks to the great teachers, the Moon beings.

As a person prepares to reenter the next earthly life, all the wisdom that preserves the past is ingrained into one's astral body. "Destiny is shaped through the fact that in the Moon existence there are beings who preserve the *past* so that it lies within us when we again set foot upon the Earth" (vol. 5, p. 22).

It is different with a Sun encounter; the Sun is negative space. It is the abode of the beings who rank immediately above humankind—angels, archangels, and archai. The gaze of the initiate is directed toward these beings in the Sun, and in this case the meeting is quite *new*. These beings have a close connection to the human being in questions (whereas in the previous case they were far away). The Sun connection reveals to the initiate "what kind of karma is about to take shape; in this case it is not old karma but karma that is coming to this person for the first time. One perceives that these beings who are connected with the Sun have to do with the *future,* just as the Moon beings have to do with the past" (vol. 5, p. 23).

> Assignment: Have you experienced times when you have had Moon or Sun encounters?

"Looking with expectation toward the future and living on into that future with our hopes and strivings, we no longer feel isolated within our own soul life, but are united with what is radiating to us from the Sun" (vol. 5, p. 24).

Organs and the cosmos

Although the human physical body disintegrates after death, something of the soul-spirit essence continues living, and the heart in particular is woven and shaped by the cosmos.

The liver on the other hand forms quite close to the stage of reincarnation on Earth. Indeed, the liver and the lungs are formed when they are in the neighborhood of the Earth. By contrast, the heart could not exist if it had not been formed over great expanses of time by the cosmos. In other words, we are close to Earth in our liver and lungs, and close to the cosmos in the functioning of the heart. As a whole, we are a microcosm of the entire universe.

Here is a transformative sequence over several incarnations:

1. Love in one incarnation can transform into the experience of joy in the next, and understanding and deep interest in nature and all world events in the third incarnation.
2. In a similar manner, when we live with hate in one incarnation, it can result in extra susceptibility to suffering in the next, and then even obtuseness in the third incarnation.

Unit 35:
Karmic Compensation and
How Destiny Takes Shape

Karmic Relationships, vol. 5, lecture 3

The third hierarchy (angels, archangels, archai) help us behold "the fruits of our attitude of mind and heart, of our life of soul, of our mode of thinking in the last earthly life.... Our attitudes, our feelings toward other individuals, toward other earthly things, are now outspread in the spiritual sphere of the universe. And we become of what our thinking and feeling signify" (vol. 5, p. 38). We learn to see that the feelings and thoughts we carried while on Earth are part of the whole world, and affect the whole world.

Pause to ponder and consider: The second hierarchy (exusiai, dynamis, kyriotetes) help us see the talents and faculties we acquired in our previous life as a result of our work, diligence, and interest in things. They cast these into mighty pictures that can then help us behold what talents and faculties will be ours in the next incarnation.

Pause to ponder and consider: The first hierarchy (seraphim, cherubim, thrones) help to reveal the consequences of our deeds in our previous life and the results they will have in the next incarnation. They help us see the effects of how we treated other people and our attitude and disposition. **"They show us, in pictures, what our experiences with individuals** with whom we had some relationship in the previous incarnation will have to become in the new relationship that will be established so that mutual compensation can be made for what happened between us in the previous life.... I myself prepare the compensatory adjustment.... These beings [of the first spiritual hierarchy] also ensure that the other individual with whom I shall again make contact is led to me in the same way as I am led to her or him" (vol. 5, p. 40).

These pictures and majestic experiences given to us as a result of the deeds of the hierarchies are recorded by the Moon beings and subsequently inscribed by them in our astral body for when the time comes for our next descent to another earthly existence. These Moon beings **"witness what is happening, so that the adjustment of the previous earthly life may take place in a subsequent life.... More and more, the longing arises in the human being for a new incarnation in which compensation can be made for what was done and experienced in a previous earthly life"** (vol. 5, p. 40).

Anthroposophy can help us awaken a new feeling, a sharpened discernment, thanks to an engagement in these spiritual matters. What was previously shadow and partially sensed aspects of human relationships can now be brought forth in the new light of understanding through the study of karma. We can see how deeply these matters affect the soul and how new strength and energy can be summoned with self-directed, compassionate work with others.

We can absorb only the spirituality and develop the constitution of soul that the body of the particular epoch allows. Behind the outer facts of history stands the quality of soul of particular human beings. [Note to reader: Further examples include Gregory VII reincarnated as Haeckel; Haroun al

Rashid came back as Lord Bacon; the counselor at court of Haroun al Rashid returned as Amos Comenius.]

Symptomatology: "**it is human souls themselves who carry the fruits of each epoch onward. We cannot understand how what appears in a later epoch has come over from an earlier one unless we perceive how the souls themselves develop onward from one epoch to the next. History is itself maya; it can be understood correctly only by getting away from maya and penetrating to the truth**" (vol. 5, p. 51).

> **Assignment:** Practice symptomatology. Select current events, identify a few key personalities involved, and look for undercurrents. What is working through them? What has influenced them? Look at their biography and childhood influences. Consider things that are larger than biographical influences and may come from an earlier life. Are there things that cannot be explained by biography alone? What is the soul constitution of the person? What kind of transformation could have led to this?

There are a number of karmic laws that can be revealed through the study of historical personalities. For example, Garibaldi, the Italian fighter for freedom, was a former Hibernian initiate. During his earlier incarnation, he had several pupils. One of the laws of initiation requires that an initiate remains loyal to former students. It so happened this was the case for Garibaldi regarding his relationship to Italian monarch Victor Emmanuel, who held values very different from the republican freedom fighter, Garibaldi. Thus two people, with very different political views were on Earth at the same time, yet bound to one another from former times: convictions and sentiments belong to the particular time in which one lives, but the laws of human connection between humans supersedes all that is transitory (vol. 5, p. 57).

> **Assignment:** Consider the difference between loyalty to people and to parties, affinity groups, particular beliefs, etc. What are the implications of this?

Rudolf Steiner described his geometry teacher and then shared the observation that "**Whatever is connected with the feet may live itself out in a subsequent incarnation in the head organization, whereas what we now bear in our head may come to expression in the organization of the legs in the later incarnation. Metamorphosis takes a peculiar form here.** One who is conversant with these things can discern from the style and manner of a person's gait (how one walks with toes and heels) the quality of thinking that characterized that person in an earlier incarnation. And one who observes the qualities of a person's thinking—whether thoughts are quick, fleeting, cursory, or deliberate and cautious—will be able to picture how that individual actually walked in a previous incarnation. In an earlier incarnation, a person whose thoughts are fleeting and cursory walked with short, rapid steps, as though tapping over the ground, whereas the gait of one who thinks cautiously and with deliberation was firm and steady in the earlier life" (vol. 5, p. 58).

> **Assignment:** Take a few days to study how people walk in light of these observations, and then try to intuit how the people around you think.

Another example of a reincarnation sequence is Lord Byron with his club foot (see vol. 5, lect. 4). A ninth-century estate owner in northeastern France went to war unsuccessfully

Unit 35: Karmic Compensation and How Destiny Takes Shape

and returned to find his house and home were now occupied by others. He was forced to live in the woods, sitting around a fire with others each night and nursing his bitter disappointments in life. He was born again in the nineteenth century as Karl Marx. This illustrates once again the transformation through multiple reincarnations. In this case, the soul experience of homelessness transformed to a passion for Marxist/Communist ideology.

Consider the connection between Mu'awiya (ca. 197–605) and Woodrow Wilson (1856–1924)—fatalism and will—and the connection between the Quran and President Wilson's fourteen points. Ordinary historical study is full of enigmas—things cannot be explained only by external facts. Spiritual investigation is needed.

In prehistoric times, people often experienced a transformation of the soul at age thirty. In ancient India, for example, people suddenly might not recognize someone they had known—"they had forgotten everything that had happened to them during the previous thirty years; they had forgotten it all—even their own identity" (vol. 5, p. 62).

There was an actual institution, and official department, or board, to which such a person would then have to apply to be told who he was and where he had been born. Only through the mysteries and special training could a few people at that time remember who they were on their own. "They were people who, at a later time, were called the twice born who owed the first period of their existence to the Moon forces, the second to the forces of the Sun.... Sun forces have to do with what a human being is able, through one's own free will, to make of oneself" (vol. 5, p. 62). Moon forces are given to us through heredity and the past.

> **Assignment:** What things have you done in your life that came from your past (family, heredity, early relationships before age thirty), and what things have you done in your life (after thirty) that have been your initiative?

Christ taught that "**When you learn to feel as I feel, when instead of turning your eyes to the Sun you behold what is alive in me—who was the very last to receive the Sun Word in the thirteenth year—then you will once again find the way to the essence of the Sun!**" (vol. 5, p. 63).

One had to sacrifice their intellect at a certain point in youth to realize the Christ as a Sun being who came to dwell in Jesus at the age of thirteen. Christianity is not merely an outer religion; it is a cosmic reality in which the Christ bears the spirituality of the Sun. Organized religion has tried to block this fact from human knowledge.

Consider the effects of illness. There was once a man with mental struggles who ultimately could not function in everyday life. This struggle became more and more extreme, ultimately reaching a point where he simply purchased train tickets anywhere and bounced from one place to another. He ended up in an asylum in Berlin where he found himself again. "**It is, in truth, the ruin of the whole 'I' when people forget what they have lived through and experienced. It would also mean the ruin of the 'I' of civilization...if people were to forget completely those things that were part of their historical experience**" (vol. 5, p. 65).

> **Assignment:** Discuss how we "forget" in our own lives but also, as a civilization, how we forget historical experiences and spiritual realities.

Unit 35: Karmic Compensation and How Destiny Takes Shape

In May 2024, I visited Robben Island in Cape Town. In addition to visiting Mandela's prison cell and the common areas, Karine and I were taken to the quarry where the prisoners worked every day. This was the only time they could speak with one another. They shared biographies, political views, and as a result, formed a brotherhood that resulted in a close-knit community in the most adverse circumstances. When they were released, it only took Mandela a few months building on these relationships to effect the overthrow of apartheid. For me, this was a powerful experience of spiritual/soul connection resulting in political change.

Unit 36:
The Journey after Death

Karmic Relationships, vol. 5, lecture 5

With the benefit of Imaginative knowledge, physical death is transformed into spiritual birth. Earth is the bearer of death in the universe: "**The whole cosmos teems with cosmic thoughts, living and weaving in the expanse of space. Having passed through death, we enter a world of cosmic thoughts—everything works and weaves in cosmic thoughts**" (vol. 5, p. 71). After death, we encounter thoughts in the *World Intelligence.* In the first days after death, there appears in the weaving of cosmic thoughts, as it were, a single cloud in which we can see the record of our past life. We see the whole of our last life as in a tableau, which then becomes increasingly faint after a few days. Our past life gradually vanishes from sight. This is accompanied by a fear that we will lose ourselves in cosmic space.

Stages after Death:

1. Stage 1: We form pictures (as seen through Imaginative Knowledge described by Rudolf Steiner).
2. Stage 2: We acquire Inspiration, which means instead of pictures we have spiritual hearing. The spiritual worlds speak to us, and we meet the beings themselves.
3. Stage 3: Then we approach the boundary of visible space and meet the stars. They are not like the physical stars we usually see; now, on our journey after death, we encounter

colonies of spiritual beings that live in the places of the stars. Once we have crossed the abyss of cosmic Intelligence, we are received into the world of stars.

In our journey after death, we encounter the Moon beings, who are the great teachers of humankind. We spend about a third of the time of our previous waking life (our time of sleep on Earth does not count). We see the days, not the nights (unless one was particularly "addicted" to sleep, it's about one third of one's time on Earth). During this time, the teachers of humanity pour their essence into us.

Karmic Reconciliation

"In the Moon sphere you experience what you did or thought during your earthly life, not as you felt it, but as it has affected the other person. After death, for a period corresponding to a third of one's lifetime, we live through, in reverse order, all that we thought and whatever wrong we did during our earthly lifetime. It is revealed to us by the Moon beings as intense reality...we become aware of how our deeds affected others. And then a strong desire arises within us as spirit man—that what we are now experiencing in the Moon sphere because of our dealings with other people on Earth may again be laid upon us, so that compensation can be made. The resolve to fulfill our destiny in accordance with our earthly deeds and earthly thoughts comes as a wish at the end of the Moon period. And if this wish (which arises from experience of the whole of earthly life back to birth) is devoid of fear, we are ready to be received into the next sphere, the Mercury sphere, into which we then pass.... In this realm, we then learn how to shape our future destiny" (vol. 5, p. 76).

Despite centuries of teachings in many religious faiths, despite the wisdom of many spiritual leaders from many countries and diverse cultures, humans on this Earth continue to inflict pain on one another. Consider recent instances such as events occurring in Sudan, Ukraine, Gaza, etc. What are the implications regarding karmic reconciliation for those on both sides of these conflicts, and those who cross the threshold of death and take the journey just described?

Unit 37: Good and Evil

Karmic Relationships, vol. 5, lecture 6

Moon beings pronounce stern judgments upon the good or bad actions of a person in the life just lived. We must leave behind in the Moon region the results of evil actions or anything in which we have done harm to the universe. "**In so doing we leave a part of our self behind. We must realize more strongly than usual that people and their deeds and achievements form a unity, that one's whole being is bound up with a good or with a bad deed. Thus, if we have to leave behind us the evil we have wrought, we also have to leave part of our self behind. In fact, we pass from this Moon region with only the good we have achieved for the universe.... Everything by which we have injured the cosmos must be left behind in the Moon region**" (vol. 5, p. 80).

The head is the most elaborately formed part of the human body, given the brain, senses etc. At death, however, when we become spiritual again, it is the head that passes away most quickly. And not just the physical aspect of the head, which of course disappears at death, but the spirit form of the head also now disappears soon after death. Those who have been mostly "good" while on Earth can now enter the Mercury sphere in a more complete way, but those who were mostly evil enter the next sphere "greatly mutilated"—less of the original individual is able to continue into the Mercury sphere (vol. 5, p. 81).

This is a challenging concept to grasp. One way to look at it is through the choices we make and the deeds we perform while on Earth. Good deeds result in a relatively "smooth passage" through the phase after death Rudolf Steiner calls the Mercury sphere. Evil deeds (and I might suggest even evil thoughts) leave us somewhat debilitated. What we have done to others comes back to "haunt" us. Steiner uses the strong term "mutilated" or "headless" in the spiritual world. And the Moon and Mercury sphere work together to also deal with health and illness:

"From the being who now appears as a headless man (if I may use this expression), all moral blemish has been removed in the Moon sphere, but not the outcome of the health or illness experienced during earthly life. This is important, for it is both significant and surprising that although we lay aside our moral blemishes in the Moon region, the spiritual effect of whatever has befallen us in the form of illness can be removed only in the Mercury region, by the beings who have never been human...the spiritual consequences of illnesses are taken away from us in the Mercury region" (vol. 5, p. 81).

> **Assignment:** Consider how you relate to the notion that the journey after death is a kind of cleansing of what happened while on Earth.

A moral blemish cannot enter the spiritual world but must remain behind in the Moon region with the beings who know the ways of human beings, because they used to live among them. However, the beings of Mercury never lived on Earth: "It is these beings who remove from us the consequences of illness. Illnesses are seen streaming out, as it were, into cosmic space; their spiritual consequences are absorbed into the spiritual cosmos.... Just as we experienced the wind, the lightning, the flow of water here on Earth, likewise, when we have passed through the gate of death and entered the Mercury region, we experience the departure of the spiritual effects of illnesses. We see how they are absorbed by the spiritual beings.... All medical knowledge, all knowledge of healing, was the secret of the Mercury mysteries" (vol. 5, p. 82). Effective medicine today either originated in ancient times (Mercury gods) or must now be rediscovered through methods to relearn how to converse with the gods. The stream of ancient wisdom has run dry, and we need a new wisdom today. "**This is the mission of Anthroposophy in all the various domains**" (vol. 5, p. 83).

Many of our achievements today, such as technology, arise from human thoughts. The judgments of the Moon beings are based on how good or bad deeds arose from thoughts.

The beings in the Mercury region continue to judge the illnesses from which they must liberate humans according to the thoughts they held. But in the next region, Venus, thoughts no longer count; everything becomes a reflection of love—love replaces wisdom. "**Human beings cannot pass into the Sun existence until love leads them into it from the sphere of wisdom**" (vol. 5, p. 83).

Unit 38: Karmic Biography

Karmic Relationships, vol. 5, lecture 6

To begin with, here is a summary of seven year stages in human biography in relation to the planetary influences as outlined by Rudolf Steiner:

Ages birth to 7: Moon mysteries
Ages 7 to 14: Mercury mysteries
Ages 14 to 21: Venus mysteries
Ages 21 to 42: beings of the Sun mysteries revealed
Ages 42 to 49: Mars mysteries
Ages 49 to 56: Jupiter mysteries
Ages 56 to 63: Saturn mysteries (see vol. 5, p. 85)

Image a circle of folding chairs in a room and notice the spaces between chairs. Then gradually take away one chair after another, until they are all gone. Now there is just space, no more "things" in the room. **Empty space is far more prevalent in the cosmos** (vol. 5, p. 87).

Another image is that when we fill a drinking glass from a bottle of sparkling Sanpellegrino water, we see little bubbles, which are less dense than water. Without the bubbles, pure water in a glass is still and clear.... Likewise, out in the cosmos, where the Sun is located, there is less than regular space—there is nothing at all, not even space. It is purely spiritual, inhabited only by spiritual beings (Steiner calls them exusiai, dynamis, kyriotetes). They can be active in this clear, spiritual condition. The greater part of life between death and a new birth is spent among the exusiai, dynamis and kyriotetes.

> **Assignment:** Consider a thought that can stretch our reflective practices: when we look back on our life after we have reached midlife, at say age forty-two, we can see a reflection of our Sun nature. What does this mean in light of the material presented in this unit and karma studies in general?

All too often "on Earth we see the good punished and the bad rewarded, for the good may be unfortunate and the bad fortunate. There seems to be no connection between moral life and physical actuality.... In the Sun existence, there are no such relationships; only *moral* relationships exist there. Everything moral in that sphere has the power of coming to realization in an appropriate way. Goodness produces phenomena that bring blessing to human beings, whereas evil brings the opposite. Here on Earth, moral relationship is only an ideal and can be established as ideal only externally and inadequately, insofar as jurisprudence sees to it that evil is punished. In the Sun region, moral relationships become reality. In this region, our every good intention, however feeble the thought, begins to become reality—a reality perceived by the exusiai, dynamis, and kyriotetes. Human beings are regarded by beings of the Sun region according to the goodness we have in us, according to the way we were able to think and feel and experience.... If, as human beings in the Earth region we have had a good thought, in the Sun region between death and a new birth, we will converse with exusiai, dynamis, and kyriotetes. We will be able to lead a spiritual life in community with those beings. If, however, we have had evil thoughts, although we left them behind in the Moon region, we will be lonely souls, abandoned by exusiai, dynamis, and kyriotetes. Thus, through community with these beings in the Sun region, goodness becomes reality. If our thoughts have not been good, we will not understand their language; if we have accomplished nothing good, we cannot appear before them. The effect of our goodness is all reality in the Sun region" (vol. 5, p. 89).

Evil falls away in the Moon sphere. The Sun sphere is pure goodness, shining, radiant goodness—it is a prolonged time between death and rebirth when we join the company of those who we knew on Earth. We also encounter the exusiai, dynamis, and kyriotetes, purely spiritual beings. "**And the moral world we behold around the Sun sphere belongs to them, just as the mineral, plant, and animal kingdoms belong to Earth**" (p. 92). In the Sun sphere the world organism is in us. Just as we have a head in earthly life, so now:

> Mars, Jupiter, and Saturn constitute our head in Sun existence—representing our intelligence.
> Mars helps us live by the cosmic word.
> Jupiter helps us bear within us the wisdom of worlds.
> Saturn gives us cosmic memory.
> The Moon, Mercury, and Venus are our limbs.
> The Sun itself is our new rhythmic system—heart and lungs.

So, the human being, while on Earth, is the bearer of all the hierarchies given to us in our pre-earthly existence. They all work in us. We are a cosmic creation. "**Look up to the Sun and say that its physical rays shining down to the Earth as warmth are the blessings bestowed by the Sun. But when** we know what the Sun is in reality, we will feel: Up yonder, where the glowing orb of the Sun moves through the universe, is the scene where the spiritual prototypes of future human generations first take shape; there the higher hierarchies work together with the human souls who lived on Earth in previous incarnations, to bring the future human beings into existence. The Sun is actually the spiritual embryo of the future earthly life. In fact, it is in the first half of the Sun existence that we spend with the gods, shaping our future Earth existence together with them" (vol. 5, p. 94).

> **Assignment:** Review the previous quotation and work backward to describe and ponder. Then read it again.

During the second half of the time in the Sun sphere, a picture is formed that will become the foundation of the physical body in the next earthly life. As we prepare for the next life, we proceed from the Sun existence through the spheres of Mars, Jupiter, and Saturn, which can be seen as a religious preparation.

From the heavens we look down into the spheres of the hierarchies and see "what will constitute the fulfillment of our karma in the next earthly life; we see what we will experience through those other individuals with whom our karma is in some way interwoven.... The gods truly are our creators, but they also create our karma.... We take our karma upon ourselves because we behold it first in the divine deeds of the seraphim, cherubim, and thrones. In this vista, we are shown what is in store for us in the next earthly life, carried into effect by the gods" (vol. 5, p. 98).

"What matters is to realize that, as human beings on the Earth in the physical body, it is incumbent upon us to become worthy of what we have brought with us from the suprasensory worlds. If knowledge becomes an impulse of will worthy of our soul life before the descent through birth, then what is taught in Anthroposophy has a direct influence" (vol. 5, p. 105).

Creating out of Nothingness: "Let us now look at the other aspect, the aspect of death that ends physical life on Earth, putting nothingness in the place of life...behind the nothingness the spiritual world of the gods rises, and human beings become conscious that they will have the strength to begin the work of forming a new physical body just where the nothingness of their former physical body has been made evident. This gives a strong and true religious impulse. And so, a picture of cosmic and human life springs from Anthroposophy. Anthroposophy is, moreover, the source from which moral and religious ideals are imbued with strength" (vol. 5, p. 106).

> **Assignment:** In a world of clutter and information overload, what is the potential for "creating out of nothingness"?

As Steiner says, we will remain united, even when physically separated.

Unit 39:
Past and Future Relationships—Moon and Sun

Karmic Relationships, vol. 6, lecture 1

The Moon and Sun are two portals through which human beings reach out beyond the Earth. In evolution, when the Moon separated from the Earth, certain beings went with it; they were of a much higher rank than human beings.

"Knowledge...is not acquired only through cleverness. Cleverness comes from the intellect, and intellect is only one of the human faculties, although nowadays it is prized more highly than all the others, especially by science. Yet, when we see how the world has developed in a moral and social respect in this enlightened twentieth century, there is really no cause to be so very proud of our intellectual culture.... If we go back and consider what originates from the ancient East, for example, we can feel only great reverence. The same may apply even to certain achievements of so-called uncivilized peoples (India and Persia), of the wonderful wisdom contained in the Vedas, in Vedanta, or in yogic philosophy. If we let these things work upon us—not superficially but with all their deep intensity—we will feel an ever-increasing reverence for what past ages created, not through cleverness as we know it, but in a very different way" (vol. 6, p. 11).

> **Assignment:** Relate this quotation to indigenous cultures in the United States and elsewhere.

In the pre-birth journey, a human being receives the influence of the Moon beings (the wise teachers). They impress upon the astral and "I" what later makes its way into the nerves and blood as a predisposition for talent, good or evil, temperament, character, and so on. In short, they give us the stamp of individuality. The Moon is **"the gate through which the past makes its way into our life and gives us individuality"** (vol. 6, p. 13). The other gateway is the Sun. It shines alike on the good and on evil people, on a genius and a fool. **"Insofar as earthly life is concerned, the Sun has no *direct* connection with our individuality"** (vol. 6, p. 13). The Christ came down from the Sun to help all human beings, regardless of nationality, class, race, or economic status. It is not the forces of the intellect but the deepest forces of the heart and soul that can receive the Christ Impulse—working not for the benefit of single individuals alone but for the universal human (because Christ is a Sun being).

Karmic reconciliation is about overcoming the Moon forces and entering the Sun space. In terms of karmic reconciliation, we need to consider what has been given to us from the past as karmic obligation: family, place of birth, group of peers in school in which we find ourselves in the early phase of life. This "given" is very much the influence of Moon as described in the Karma lectures.

But we need to overcome karmic obligation and seek out karmic fulfillment which often happens in the middle period of life, ages 28 to 56. That is when we find ourselves in a place of work, teachers and parents find themselves in community, and there are opportunities to resolve and fulfill what has been given from the past, and then in the last decades of a person's life, we have a chance to work out of karmic sacrifice, free deeds that can help humans further evolve. These last phases are very much connected to the influence of Sun. (More detail on this subject can be found in the appendix in the article Karmic Leadership.)

The past is ruled by Moon forces, but we are connected to our future through the Sun existence. The intellect is connected to the brain, the Sun influence to the heart. The Sun forces call on us to reach out beyond our own limitations. Our temperaments are an interplay of Sun and Moon, playing into the physical and etheric. Melancholia has a stronger influence of the Moon, and sanguine is more of the Sun. Phlegmatic is more of a balance between the two. The physical body is continually cast off; it is in a stream from within outward. Many people today understand the physical and draw conclusions that are "correct but not true" (p. 16). What endures between birth and death is the soul, and what endures in the celestial bodies is a multiplicity of beings.

"We can never alter the past...the Moon forces lay hold of our human nature [and are a force] of immutable *necessity*.... Whatever comes from the Sun and points to the future, there is something in which our will, our *freedom* can be a factor" (vol. 6, p. 17). "Necessity and freedom interweave in our destiny. In terms of the terrestrial and human, we speak of necessity and freedom; in terms of the heavenly and cosmic, we speak of Moon existence and Sun existence" (vol. 5, p. 18).

"If we begin to think about our relationship to some human being we seem to have met quite by accident, we will have to say to ourselves that we had been looking for that person, seeking for him or her ever since we were born into earthly existence...and, as a matter of fact, even before then.... There is, however, a significant difference between what takes place before the actual meeting of two individuals and what takes place from that moment onward. Before they met in earthly life, they influenced each other without having any knowledge of the other's existence. After the meeting, the mutual influence continues, but now they know each other. And this, again, is the beginning of something extremely significant" (vol. 6, p. 19).

> **Assignment:** Consider whether you have had such an experience.

What is at work *before* they actually meet in earthly life is determined by the Moon. What takes place *after* their meeting is determined by the Sun. Thus, the former is the outcome of necessity; the latter is the expression of freedom—"mutually free relationship and behavior" (vol. 6, p. 20). The weaving of the two influences makes up our karma, or destiny.

Two kinds of relationships often exist between human beings: some proceed from the *will*, and others more from the *intellect* or from an aesthetic sense. With some we just interact, perhaps feel some sympathy or antipathy or a passing acquaintance. With other people, we want to connect and get involved, see the person as a role model that engages our will. "**Our relationship to a human being is deeper if, as soon as we meet, we begin to dream about him or her**" (p. 21). With some, we meet, listen, and then go our way with little or no further engagement. With others, we listen, and when we go on our way it's as if they are still speaking to us, to our inner being!

"When we meet other human beings who have no effect on our will—of whom we do no more than form a judgment—there is no strong karmic connection between us; we have had little to do with them in earlier earthly lives. Individuals who deeply affect our will, so that they always seem to be with us—whose form is so strongly impressed upon us that they are always in our thoughts, so that we dream of them even in our waking life—are individuals with whom we have had a great deal to do in past earthly lives, with whom we are, as it were, cosmically connected through the gate of the Moon. Whereas in our present life we are connected through the Sun with everything that lives in us without any element of the necessity belonging to Moon existence. Thus, destiny is woven" (vol. 6, p. 22).

As the bearer of the intellect, our brain is independent of our individuality. Because of this, through thoughts we are able to connect to others and find mutual understanding. The intellect is a universal principle. Things that happen in the *present*, such as meeting someone, work on the intellect. Things that are not part of our karma work on the intellect. All that has karmic links resulting from past experiences once shared lies in the will. "**The will is at work even before we actually meet a human being with whom we are karmically connected.**... The karma that brings two human beings together is shrouded in the deepest obscurity of all. They become dimly aware that karma is at work by the way their wills are involved. The moment they come face to face the intellect begins to work, and what is then woven by the intellect can become the basis of future karma.... For two human beings who are karmically connected, their karma has worked itself out once the meeting has taken place. What they may do after that as a continuation of what lives in the unconscious—that, and that alone, becomes part of the stream of future karma. But a great deal is then woven into their destiny, which affects only the intellect and its sympathies and antipathies. Past and future, Moon existence and Sun existence intermingle here. The thread of karma that reaches into the past is interwoven with the thread that reaches into the future" (vol. 6, p. 24).

Our destiny is an image of the world of stars, of Sun and Moon. We can see the universe and read the scroll of our human life. Likewise, we can learn to look into our own soul and understand the world through it. Necessity and freedom are at work in each human being.

UNIT 40:
HUMAN ENCOUNTERS

Karmic Relationships, vol. 6, lectures 2-4

Anthroposophy must be *practiced*. Great secrets and enigmas of historical evolution can be revealed when we ponder ways that individuals have carried impulses over from one epoch to another. **"It is the *Trinity* that makes it possible for the *impulse of freedom* to have its place in the evolution of Christianity"** (vol. 6, p. 35). The Father/Mother principle is behind everything that places the human being from birth onward onto Earth (a creative act through the Moon forces). The Hebrews valued the Father-God impulse—all that is predetermined through their ancestors and the forces of nature.

Consider the Indian epoch and how many people lost all memory at age thirty, when the soul was completely transformed. A person would begin a new existence through the guidance of the mysteries. This was the secret of the Sun. What is reborn in the human being is *not predetermined* by the Moon forces but rather what is transformed (vol. 6, pp. 39–41).

The Sun and Moon are dwelling places of spiritual beings. They also dwell in connection with other celestial bodies, but they have less influence on humans between death and rebirth. The Sun is connected to our "I," the Moon with our astral body.

In primeval ages on Earth, human beings were encouraged to maintain *complete stillness* and calm in their souls at certain times and shut out their physical environment so that the great teachers could speak within them. This was experienced as Inspiration and sometimes resulted in great works of wisdom, bearing the fruits of this inspiration in language that was half poetry. The sages could then teach humans through these inspirations. Fragments of these teachings remain today in the Vedic literature, yoga, and Vedanta philosophy of India, the lore of ancient Persia, Egypt, and so on. But then human beings outgrew this primal wisdom so they could reach new maturity through freedom in knowledge achieved through their own efforts. Today, the wisdom preserved on the Moon can be investigated when humans develop higher faculties through working with exercises such as those in Steiner's book, *How to Know Higher Worlds*.

"The Moon beings keep the 'books,' or records, of the whole past of humanity and of each individual. These books are not, of course, anything in the least like the volumes in our libraries, but this designation is nevertheless justifiable. These 'books' contain records of what all individual human beings have experienced in their successive earthly lives. As we descend from the cosmos to Earth from the existence stretching between death and a new birth, we come into inner contact with the records of our past in these great 'books' kept by the Moon sages. Before we arrive on the Earth, this past is imprinted in the astral body we bring with us into earthly existence, and in that astral body are the 'entries' made by the Moon beings" (vol. 6, p. 51).

"What is inscribed into human beings during the final stage of descent from the cosmos to Earth is inscribed into the part of us we call the spiritual side of the metabolic-limb system. The inscriptions therefore lie deep down in the unconscious, but they are actually there and pass over into the growth process and the health, and above all they determine what I will call the 'curability' [*Heilbarkeit*] of human beings when they are ill on Earth. It is clearly important to understand the nature of illness, and even more important to understand how to heal. Suprasensory knowledge itself is an essential help, for it reveals what has been inscribed from the akasha chronicle by the Moon beings into the forces involved in the process of breathing, and so on. It is these inscriptions that determine whether we put up strong or only slight resistance to the healing of an illness. One individual will be easily healed, another only with difficulty. This depends entirely on how the karma from previous earthly lives makes it possible for the inscriptions to take effect" (vol. 6, p. 52).

> **Assignment:** Discuss this quotation in relation to the Hippocratic oath, which requires a doctor to do no harm and everything possible to heal. Yet, Steiner said that a doctor must not interfere with a patient's karma (see Steiner's *Understanding Healing*).

The Sun is where the angels live, one of whom is connected to each individual human being. What we have done in the past works on into our present life, so the present works on into the future. **"But this is possible only through the angeloi, who direct their gaze toward a person's present deeds and bring them to effect in the future"** (vol. 6, p. 55).

The more we use definite and vivid imagery when working with our angel, the more our deeds will bear abundant fruit in the future.

With heightened faculties of perception, we can see in the light of the full moon our own past destiny. In the new moon, the dark shadow can become the great admonisher formed by destiny, proclaiming what our attitude must be toward actions in a previous earthly life, "so that human beings may compensate for them in the further course of their karma" (vol. 6, p. 56). The Sun can help us gain an inkling of future destinies, in general and without specific details.

"Entries made by the Moon beings in the akasha chronicle influenced the paths taken by [two people]. From the moment they meet, the subconscious is no longer all-important, for the two now come face to face and make a certain impression on each other. This is not a matter of conserving the past; it is the *present* that is now at work. The angeloi intervene and lead the individuals concerned to further stages. The forces of Sun existence are now operating, so that within their inmost being, Sun and Moon together weave their destiny" (vol. 6, p. 56).

"When two individuals meet, the impression they make upon each other may be intrinsically different. There are cases in which one of the two takes the other right into the sphere of her or his will and feelings. The outer, personal impression has had little influence here.... The origin of the bond between the two lies in experiences they shared in the previous life...the working of the will would indicate that past earthly lives have already been spent in company with such individuals; moreover, subconscious soul forces give hints of experiences shared with others in the past incarnations" (vol. 6, p. 57).

"If the effect made by the two upon each other reaches into the will, into the heart, into the inmost nature, then a karmic connection exists; the two individuals have been led to each other as the result of common experiences in the past earthly life. If an effect made by another person reaches only into the intellect, the aesthetic sense, this is not a result of the Moon's activity, but a situation brought about by the Sun and one that will have its sequel only in the future. And so, through a thoughtful, observant study of human life we can learn to perceive the signs of karmic connections" (vol. 6, p. 58).

> **Assignment:** Make a list of people you have known, with examples of each of the foregoing possibilities:
>
> - People who have impressed us deeply, affected our will, reached into the heart, our innermost nature. We might even dream about the person.
> - People who we have met and who we find interesting intellectually or attract interest by virtue of outer appearance—aesthetic impression, verbal skills—but did not affect or move us deeply.

The goal is to be able to hear the *inner* voice as well as the outer when someone is talking to us, to hear the spiritual speech behind the words. When meeting someone new, someone with whom there is no karmic bond, an initiate can hear clear and definite speech... one hears what the angel of a particular person is saying.

"When you go to a tea party or some such function, just keep your ears open and listen to the conversation. If a person has met another individual with whom he or she is karmically connected, the person will say little about the others who are present, but about this particular individual the person will say something of real significance, especially if unaware of what is behind it all. At the same kind of tea party, you may get into conversation with someone with whom you have no karmic connection at all. Your interest in the person is very superficial and seems to you to be typical of all the other guests. Such a gathering is very brief as a rule, and a great deal of talk goes on about world affairs, about noted politicians and the like. After listening to these few people, we might judge the whole of society by this criterion. The judgment may be erroneous but nevertheless it is through individuals with whom we have no karmic connection that another aspect of the world is presented to us" (vol. 6, p. 63).

"We are united inwardly with those with whom we were associated in the previous earthly life. In the future, people must develop a delicate feeling for the stirring of the will when meeting another person. In about seven to nine thousand years, all human beings on Earth will be able to hear those with whom they are karmically connected, speaking from within" (vol. 6, p. 60).

Akashic pictures are *living pictures:* When looking at a portrait of a person, an initiate might even recognize a previous incarnation of that individual. "The light radiating to us from the Moon is connected with our cosmic *past*, and the light of the Sun is connected with our cosmic *future*" (vol. 6, p. 64).

> **Assignment:** Do meditations on Sun and Moon, nature experiences, and journaling.

Lecture 4 took place in Stuttgart as a version of much of earlier material: "Suppose two people who have never seen each other before meet at a particular moment. From this moment, something that is a result of joint action begins to play a part in their lives. Their recognition of each other is mutual, and they know that from now on they will have a great deal to do with each other. If two people in this situation review the course of their lives since childhood, they will find, if they observe with sufficient detachment, that everything they did up to the moment of their meeting had a definite significance, in that every step they took since childhood seems from the beginning to have been so cleverly directed that the path led them to the point where the meeting took place. If, starting from the time when they met and began to form a friendship, they look back over their past lives without preconceived notions, it will seem that since a certain starting point in their distant childhood, every step led them inevitably to the place where they finally met. Whatever they did purposefully was of course done unconsciously; the conscious period began only after the meeting, but the conscious and the unconscious unite in a remarkable way. In the weaving of our destiny there is a great difference between the path we have arranged unconsciously so that we may meet the other person, and what we do after the meeting has taken place. Then that person is actually before us, we understand what the person says, and we adjust our actions to what he or she is doing in external life; we lead a common life, of which our senses and intellect are aware. But we shall see how that common life is interwoven with what we did until the time we met. We may well ask: What is it that is taking effect in all these forces and movements that finally bring us together?" (vol. 6, p. 70).

> Assignment: Apply this to concrete situations—a job interview, colleagueship, neighbor relations, etc. Discuss.

On illness: "In itself, our organism is healthy, for it is born out of its healthy "I," healthy astral body, and healthy etheric world. When someone becomes ill here on Earth, it can be only because something approaches from outside that, owing to the inherent constitution, that person is unable to transform completely [using an example of a warm or cold room]. We cannot take anything from the environment of the Earth into ourselves without transforming it—this also applies to the food we eat. We transform what we eat, just as we transform everything in the environment.... If no transformation is achieved, we fall ill. Here lies the physical cause of illness, but illness can also be connected with destiny.... The karmic aspect of illness is carried over from previous earthly lives into our present life, because we admitted into ourselves in earlier incarnations elements that are not fit for human beings; we have become susceptible to illness. These ideas and impressions work in this present life as potent causes of illness. Something that may have been no more than an idea or inner experience of the soul in one earthly life is transformed in the period we live through between death and rebirth into forces that work physically" (vol. 6, pp. 78–79).

Unit 41:
The Role of Historical Personalities in the Study of Karma

Karmic Relationships, vol. 6, lectures 5–7

After giving examples of Haroun al Raschid, Bacon, and Comenius, Rudolf Steiner offers an intriguing thought: Initiates who reincarnate do so into the conditions of the physical body and education they are given *in a new life. In many cases, our current form of education makes it very hard for returning initiates:* "for a long time now, the character of education has made it impossible for what once lived in these initiate-souls to express itself" (vol. 6, p. 92).

Furthermore, Rudolf Steiner made a statement on the incarnations of women and why they are not featured more in his historical examples: "Incarnations as women are only now beginning to be of importance, although in the future it will be of very special interest to take account of them" (vol. 6, p. 97). Many of the people Steiner mentions had intervening incarnations as women who were important for the further development of the souls in question, yet outer history has not, until recently, begun to focus adequately on the lives of women (as with the late adoption of the Nineteenth Amendment in 1920 and the right to vote).

Looking at socioeconomic implications of reincarnation, Steiner shares an example I find particularly intriguing. He asks us to consider a sequence in which a wealthy landowner returns from war and finds that his estate has been taken over by someone else. As a result he is forced to become a serf on his own land! Naturally, he experiences much resentment and spends many evenings in conversation with other serfs around their campfires in the woods. Steiner then says that after a journey through death, these two individuals return to Earth in a next life as Marx and Engels (vol. 6, p. 99).

Another example Rudolf Steiner offers involves a successor to Prophet Mohammed in the seventh century, Mu'awiya, who then reincarnated as Woodrow Wilson. In a striking claim, he states that much of the phrasing of Wilson's famous fourteen points for peace (given at the end of World War I) are similar to passages in the Quran (vol. 6, p. 100).

Lucifer and Ahriman

People can easily go astray if pulled in either direction: Those with an Ahrimanic disposition can go about the day as if in a swoon, a kind of paralysis. Those who have a Luciferic disposition will go through the day with a confused consciousness, with thoughts and feelings in a perpetual jumble. But we are usually protected by the Guardian of the Threshold during sleep, without which our experiences every night would be unendurable.

Steiner then indicates how the journey after death can help with healing. While a person is on the journey after death, a resolve is made: "**Owing to this and that, you have become imperfect, you are an inferior human being; and you must make compensation! Thereby, a plan of karma is laid down. And such resolutions in the spiritual world between death and a new birth are** *realities.* **Just as here on Earth it is a reality that you burn yourself if you put your finger into a flame, so it is a reality in the spiritual world**

Unit 41: The Role of Historical Personalities in the Study of Karma

when you form a resolution. And you do most assuredly form it!" (vol. 6, p. 107).

"In the Mercury sphere, human being are freed from all the effects that illnesses have produced upon one's soul. Therefore, it happens that true medicine can be mastered only when one is able to perceive how the dead are freed from illnesses in the Mercury sphere. This teaches us what must be done for human beings on Earth to free them from illnesses" (vol. 6, p. 108).

We spend the longest time in the Sun-existence. In the first period we work on the prototype of the future *physical* corporality, and in the second half on the prototype of one's *moral nature*. We work on our karma together with the beings of the planetary systems (vol. 6, p. 110). Previous incarnations of Schiller (vol. 6, pp. 111–13) had a strong Saturn stage in pre-birth journey, and Goethe (vol. 6, pp. 114–15) had a strong Jupiter influence.

It is interesting to contemplate that Rudolf Steiner presented his karma lectures in 1924 (*as well as* the class lessons for the School of Spiritual Science), when in his own life he was around 65, since he also observes: **"Truth to tell, until they have passed the sixty-third year of life, even initiates cannot see the circumstances of life between death and a new birth in which Saturn plays a part"** (vol. 6, p. 113).

Steiner also describes the Platonic and Aristotelian streams in history and the fact that **"those human beings who come to the anthroposophic movement through their karma are predestined for this movement"** (vol. 6, p. 123).

He describes a great "cosmic ritual" at the end of the nineteenth century in which souls were drawn together by experiences they had through long, long ages. There were two main groups:

1. The Platonists who then came back as early Christians after Golgotha, and then in a third incarnation as members of the School of Chartres, mostly Cistercians.
2. Aristotelians who emphasized more the development of the intellect and then came back as pre-Christian. Then in a third cycle they returned as Scholastics, and Dominicans (vol. 6, pp. 136–40).

The result of this convergence of the two streams is greater unification on Earth today: **"The aim of the Anthroposophical Society is to unite these two elements"** (vol. 6, p. 138).

Unit 42:
The Age of Michael

Karmic Relationships, vol. 6, lectures 8 and 9

Evolution is a constant process in all of humanity: Angels work with individual human beings; archangels work with groups of human beings.

The Age of Gabriel rules over the realm of *physical* forces and has to do with *births* and spiritual processes underlying propagation. The Age of Michael has to do with the *spiritual* element in culture through sciences, arts, etc. Every 2,000 years the cycle of the archangels repeats itself, but on a different basis. Gabriel is always preparatory to an age during which people are more separated and differentiated, and nationalism finds expression in the next epoch of Michael.

The Michaelic age features a longing in humankind "to overcome racial distinctions and to spread through all the peoples living on Earth the highest and most spiritual form of culture produced by the particular age—*cosmopolitanism*—spiritual impulses received by people **"no matter what language they speak"** (vol. 6, p. 145). Michael dwells on the Sun, where he administers cosmic intelligence.

External history is always accompanied by spiritual streams working less visibly. The battle today is laid in the *human heart.*

An example given by Steiner involves the invention of printing, which brings with it spiritual qualities and can become the soil of demonic powers when misused. We must "ennoble the art of printing through our reverence for the Michael wisdom. Ahriman is intent upon conquest of intelligence. These ahrimanic spirits take possession of human consciousness; they entrench themselves within it" (vol. 6, p. 174). An example is the outbreak of World War I and the lowering of consciousness among many world leaders.

When Europeans arrived in North America with books, indigenous peoples "saw these volumes with their strange characters of script [and] they took the letters to be little demons. They had the right perception for these things. They were terribly frightened when they looked at all those little demonic entities—*a, b,* and the rest, as they appear in print" (vol. 6, p. 174).

"Human hearts must become the helpers of Michael in conquering the Intelligence that has fallen to the Earth. Just as once the old serpent was destined to be crushed by Michael, so must the Intelligence that has now become the serpent be conquered by Michael— spiritualized by Michael. And whenever the serpent appears in its non-spiritualized state, made ahrimanic, it must be recognized through the vigilance and alertness that belongs to the anthroposophic spirit and is developed through the Michael-like tenor of soul" (vol. 6, p. 179).

> **Assignment:** How can we become more and more vigilant, awake, aware? How can we develop the eyes to see beyond the presenting phenomena of current events? Discuss with a group.

Unit 43:
Planetary Influences in Human Life

Karmic Relationships, vol. 7, lectures 1 and 2

A corpse indicates that something has died. Likewise, our pre-earthly thinking dies on Earth: "**Abstract thinking is the corpse of what was once *living thinking*"** (vol. 7, p. 12). Our physical body is the grave of pre-earthly living thinking, which has been entombed in the physical body. "**The spiritual in humankind dies through birth; the physical part of a human being dies through death**" (vol. 7, p. 12).

"Our stream of destiny issues from ourselves.... We form an inner urge from one life to another, and we place ourselves in a position to experience events and other people. The great teachers move in the etheric bodies of humans in pre-birth existence, and they guide and lead the soul. In ancient times, one still felt them while on Earth as inspiration, a flashing up of truth, or visions. People heard these teachings rising from within and said, 'One of the great primeval teachers of humanity has now drawn near to me'... they even felt something that was like a spiritual grasp of the hand" (vol. 7, p. 15). But human freedom would not have been possible if the primeval teachers had remained among humankind. So now we just meet these great teachers shortly after we cross through the gate of death.

"The first seed of karma is formed out of the experiences we undergo after death in the realm of the great primeval teachers of humanity. For there we resolve to make compensation for what we have done. Resolves, intentions, here take actual effect. On Earth, the good does not always seem to be followed by good, nor evil by evil. But the resolutions made in a world of far greater reality than the earthly world, the experiences for which we ourselves must make compensation—such resolutions will lead in a later life to actual adjustment. It is my intention to describe to you how karma gradually takes shape for a new life when—having lived through the time between death and rebirth—one appears again in another incarnation. During the first period after death, through communion with the Moon beings, we form the resolve to fulfil our karma" (vol. 7, p. 20).

"Through the sacred rites enacted in these mysteries, spiritual beings were able to come down from the Mercury sphere to the altars in the sanctuaries where the priests of the mysteries conversed with them. The beings who thus descended to the altars were known to the mysteries simply as the *God Mercury*. The influence was the same, although it was not necessarily the same beings who descended on every occasion. The human attitude toward this sacred medicine in ancient times was such that they said: 'The art of healing has been imparted by the God Mercury to his priest healers'" (vol. 7, p. 24).

When we pass through the Moon and Mercury spheres, we cast off weaknesses due to wrongdoing and illnesses. Thus, we are no longer whole, since those wrongdoings were part of us. "We are one with, identical with, what is evil in us according to the standards of the spiritual world. Therefore, when we arrive at the Venus sphere, we have been mutilated in a certain respect. In the Venus sphere the element of purest love prevails—purest love in the spiritual sense; and it is the cosmic love that carries what now remains of the human being from the Venus sphere into the Sun existence. There, in the Sun existence, we have to work in a very real way at the molding and shaping of our karma" (vol. 7, p. 25).

On Sun, there are cosmic laws that give effect to the karmic consequences of the Good and operate in "restoring the mutilation we have experienced as the result of our 'bad' karma when we have been transported by the love of the Venus beings into the Sun sphere" (vol. 7, p. 26).

"And now, picture to yourselves a certain inner relationship that might exist between one person and another and comes to physical expression. Picture it quite graphically. You are caressed by someone who loves you. You feel the caress, but it would be childish to associate it in any way with physical matter. The caress is not matter at all; it is a process, and you experience it inwardly, in the *soul*. So it is when we look outward into the spheres of the ether. The gods in their love caress the world, but the caress lasts long, because the life of the gods spans immense reaches of time. In truth, stars are the expression of love in the cosmic ether; there is nothing physical about them. And from the cosmic aspect, to see a star means to feel a caress that has been prompted by love. To gaze at the stars is to become aware of the love proceeding from the divine spiritual beings" (vol. 7, p. 28).

Biographical stages and planetary influences (also earlier):

Moon	birth–7
Mercury	7–14
Venus	14–21
Sun	21–42
Mars	42–49
Jupiter	49–56
Saturn	56–63

Planets are the builders and shapers of human destiny, the cosmic timepiece according to which we live out our karma. Together, they form a cosmic alphabet (vol. 7, pp. 30–35).

Unit 44:
Unity

Karmic Relationships, vol. 7, lectures 3 and 4

"Here on Earth, we say 'my heart'—meaning something that is inside our skin. Between death and a new birth, we do not say 'my heart,' but 'my Sun,' for at a certain stage between death and rebirth, when our being has expanded into the universe, the Sun is within us, just as here on Earth the heart is within us—and the same applies in a spiritual sense to the rest of the starry worlds, as I have described. Conversely, what was enclosed within our skin on Earth now becomes our outer world. But do not imagine that it bears any resemblance to what an anatomist sees when dissecting a corpse. The spectacle is even grander and more majestic than the panorama of the universe presented to us on Earth. From the vantage point of our life between death and a new birth, a whole world is revealed in what the physical senses perceive merely as heart, lung, liver, and so forth; it is a world greater and more impressive than the outer universe at which we gaze during life on Earth.... The secret lies in the fact that, first, all those human beings with whom we have karmic ties are seen as a unity, as one world. Then there are the other souls who also form a unified though less-defined whole. This host of souls is linked to those with whom we have actual karmic ties, and again there is a unified whole. The moment we pass from the physical world into the spiritual world, everything is different.... In the physical world we can count—one, two, three...we can also count money, although perhaps not just at the present time, but counting does not really mean anything in the spiritual world. Number has no particular significance there; everything is more or less a unity. If things are to be counted, they must be distinct and separate from one another, and this does not apply in the spiritual world" (vol. 7, pp. 38–39).

On Earth, when dealing with trauma or disassociation, we are encouraged to count, clap hands, and so on to keep us grounded. In the spiritual world everything is reunited; there is no need for separation.

> **Assignment:** Discuss the process of whole to parts and back to whole.

"From the vantage point of the spiritual world, whatever is *within* us in the physical world presents a very different appearance. Human structure is even more splendid, more awe-inspiring than the structure of the heavens as perceived from the Earth" (vol. 7, p. 39). "The substance of the physical body is continuously changing" (vol. 7, p. 39), every seven years a complete change. You, the reader, were completely different, physically, seven years ago! What has remained the same is your individuality, your spirit-soul. We inherit our *model* of a physical body from our parents, but by the time of change of teeth the body has been transformed.

Similar transformations occur on the journey after death. For example, after moving through the planetary spheres of Moon, Mars, Mercury, and so on, we enter the second half of our Sun journey, when the impulse to live out our karma is kindled: "Through the whole time we gaze at the earthly realm below, where our karma must take effect, gaze at it longingly, as something to which all our forces of feeling are directed—just as here on Earth, between birth and death, we gaze upward with longing toward the heavens.... In suprasensory realms, our karma is lived through in advance by the seraphim, cherubim, and thrones. In truth, the gods are the creators of the earthly. They live through everything in advance in the realm of spirit; then, in the physical realm it comes to fulfilment" (vol. 7, pp. 41–42).

> **Assignment:** What are the implications of above? Preparation in the spiritual world, "on Earth as it is in heaven."

> NOTE TO READER: For further examples of reincarnation, read what Steiner says regarding these individuals (vol. 7, pp. 44–50):
>
> - Indian initiate with poor eyesight—Heinrich Heine
> - Person versed in Manichean-Cabbalistic doctrines—Voltaire
> - Sculptor in ancient Greece—Goethe
> - Person immersed in Mexican mysteries—Éliphas Lévi]

This image illustrates the influence of the Saturn phase of our journey between death and a new birth: "**Imagine yourselves walking about the Earth, never knowing in the immediately present moment what you are doing, what you are thinking, what is happening to you or through you; you are just walking.** As you walk you do not see yourselves, but you leave traces behind; from the spot you reached a moment previously there arises, let us say, a little snowman; you take another step—another little snowman is there; a further step—again a little snowman...and so it goes on. Mobile figures are being left behind you all the time, and you can look back and see yourself exactly as you once were. The very moment something has happened through you, you see it there—see how it remains and becomes part of eternity. You look back, and from this perspective see everything that has happened through you inscribed, as it were, in an eternal chronicle in the universe. The consciousness of the Saturn beings is of this character... they gaze back upon the memory (if I may express it so) of all the beings of the whole planetary system. Everything is inscribed in this faculty of cosmic remembrance, cosmic memory, of the Saturn beings" (vol. 7, pp. 52–53).

"The Saturn sphere has a deep and incisive effect upon the shaping of karma.... [It] works in such a way that the forces will penetrate deeply, very deeply, into the physical organization.... The result is a physical organization that strives for a balancing out of the experiences undergone by the soul in an earlier earthly life. The element of retrospection is always at work. When our karma is being wrought out in the Saturn sphere, we look backward to remembrances in the past. Then, when we come down to the earthly realm, the negative images, as it were, of what we have lived through in the Saturn sphere disclose themselves. The intense concentration on the past is transformed into a resolve, striving for ideals that lead forward, toward the *future*" (vol. 7, p. 54).

> **Assignment:** How can we transform impulses of the past into ideals of the future, especially given the troubled nature of so many earthly experiences?

Steiner struggled with spelling even at age fifteen. He mentions how indigenous people in America reacted to seeing the writing of Europeans—frightened by little demons on the page. In Waldorf schools, many teachers feel it is unnatural to introduce young children to spelling, reading, and such too early (vol. 7, p. 57).

"It is not in external similarities that we must seek for evidence of the working of karma; rather we must be observant of the things that, in the deep foundations of a person's being, are carried over through karma from one earthly life into another. Perception of the karma of an individual human being, or even of one's own karma, requires the right attitude, the right mood of soul.... The mood in which all teachings about karma should be received is one of piety, reverence. Whenever human beings approach a truth relating to karma, their souls should feel as though part of the veil of Isis were being lifted.... 'I am what was, is, and will be'" (vol. 7, p. 62).

> **Assignment:** Discuss questions such as:
>
> - If soul experiences in one life lead to transformed soul-physical characteristics in the next, how can we learn to perceive in the human form the working of past karma?
> - In this age of sensory overstimulation, multitasking, and distraction, how can we find sanctuary in everyday life and begin to rediscover the piety and reverence needed for a study of karma that can lift the veil concealing insight?
> - In ancient times, this was cultivated in temples of higher learning. How can we find etheric temples for this work?

Unit 45:
Where do we belong? Who are our people?

Karmic Relationships, vol. 7, lecture 5

Studying karmic connections and historical personalities can shed light on details of our own karma. "The clear and distinct feeling for karma is a preparation for clairvoyant insight. This feeling and perception can play a part in the life of every individual, provided that one is not concerned exclusively with superficialities and outwardly sensational happenings but develops a sensitive understanding of the more intimate experiences of existence and an inkling of certain connections of destiny" (vol. 7, p. 64).

> **Assignment:** How do we balance the "superficialities and outwardly sensational happenings" in life with the contemplative, intimate experiences along the journey? Journal and/or discuss.

"A great deal depends upon how we are placed into existence as children. The faculties that are drawn out of us, the paths along which we are directed—all this has infinite significance for the destiny of our whole life. Later on, as independent human beings, we can of course take a hand in directing our own existence, but even then, the place assigned to us in childhood is determinative. And so, if we observe closely, we will certainly be able to perceive how destiny plays into our free actions, our free deeds and activities" (vol. 7, p. 65).

Unit 45: Where do we belong? Who are our people?

> **Assignment:** Consider the importance of these thoughts in regard to early childhood, especially birth to 3, and the role of parents in Waldorf schools.

We respond in one of two ways to our human encounters:

1. **Reactive:** We respond to a person with feelings of sympathy or antipathy, even in that person's presence. We are drawn to the person and it does not depend on outer appearance. Affection may arise, even if only through professional kinship. With this person, we have some past karma and experiences that have shaped our feelings and attitudes. We even dream about this person.
2. **Proactive:** We meet someone and want to discover who that person is. What does this person think? Is this individual friendly or not? Who might be our mutual acquaintances? We feel as if we have been thrown together and are not sure why. We share a current circumstance with this person (job, neighborhood, new family relation, and so on). Although karma is certainly at work here, it is only *the beginning*, just starting to form and in a process of coming into being. These are current relationships *that are starting to form future karma*.

> **Assignment:** Make two lists, one for each type of relationship you have had in life thus far. Compare with others and discuss.

There is a karmic law which states **"Individuals who have been together in an earthly life in which karma begins to form will endeavor in the next earthly life to find their way to each other again. Once again, they will establish karmic links—will again pass through the life between them and again** seek a common earthly existence. And here, the remarkable fact comes to light that, as Earth's evolution runs its course, human beings live together in groups" (vol. 7, p. 67).

> **Assignment:** Consider the implications for a Waldorf school faculty, college, board/trust, a group of parents in a particular class and so on.

The Waldorf School as a Karmic Community!

Given some of the thoughts found in *Karmic Leadership* [see appendix], it is interesting to work with a personal comment Steiner made about himself. He would have loved to be a contemporary of Goethe, but, **"To have been a contemporary of Goethe would have made it impossible to keep one's own disposition and configuration of soul firmly in hand.... When karma is interpreted rightly, it becomes a source of strength in the circumstances of our life, establishing us in earthly existence in the place where we truly belong"** (vol. 7, p. 69).

UNIT 46:
MEMORIES

Karmic Relationships, vol. 7, lectures 6 and 7

In our thinking we are awake; in our feelings we dream; in our will we are in perpetual sleep.

"We feel that in this earthly life we *are* what we can remember.... You will realize from this how closely our 'I' is bound up with our store of memories. We know nothing of the self within us if we are lacking the store of memories...memories are of the nature of *soul*" (vol. 7, pp. 82–83).

An example is given of a person who gradually lost his memory and continually bought train tickets to travel aimlessly, until he suddenly regained full consciousness and found himself in a group home in Berlin. [Note to reader: for further reading, please consider the stories found in *Memory Wall* by Anthony Doerr. This account is set in Cape Town, South Africa, and includes many insights on race relations.]

"From this delicate, intimate observation of the bodily development of a child between the seventh and fourteenth years, there can arise the faculty to gaze into the life preceding the descent to earthly existence, the life between death and a new birth" (vol. 7, p. 86).

> **Assignment:** Consider the implications for teachers of the previous quotation. Can we learn to sense the *journey of descent* prior to birth? How could that help us connect with our students better and teach a curriculum that truly speaks to them?

Riddle: "Nevertheless, there *is* such a thing as selfless love, and it is within our reach. We can learn little by little to expel every vestige of self-interest from love, and we then come to know what it means to give ourselves to others in the true and real sense. It is from this self-giving—giving ourselves to others, selfless love—that we can kindle the feeling that must arise if we are to glimpse earlier earthly lives.... Two personalities are linked by the life stretching between death and the new birth. But before even so much as an inkling can come to you of the personality who lived in the eighth century, you must be capable of loving your own self exactly as if you were loving another human being. For although the being who lived in the eighth century is there within you, that person is really a stranger, exactly as another person might be a stranger to you now. You must be able to relate yourself to your preceding incarnation in the way you now relate yourself to some other human being; otherwise, no inkling of the earlier incarnation is possible. Nor will you be able to form an objective concept of what appears in a human being after puberty as a second, shadowy person. But love that is truly selfless becomes a power of knowledge, and when love of self becomes so completely objective that we can observe ourselves exactly as we observe other human beings, this is the means whereby a vista of earlier earthly lives will disclose itself—at first as a kind of dim inkling.... 'I am striving to apprehend the *whole* human being, the being who has passed through many earthly lives. I am striving to know what it is within me that has come from earlier stages of existence'" (vol. 7, pp. 89–90).

> **Assignment:** Let us take the foregoing step by step.
>
> - What is selfless love?
> - How can we learn to love ourselves?
> - What does it mean to see the other objectively?
> - See ourselves (in a former life) with objective love?
> - What in me has come from an earlier life?

We need to study historical personalities to gain perception of our own individual karma (such as Haroun al Raschid and his wise counselor—Lord Bacon and Comenius).

We will not be up to dealing with world events until we have learned to study karma and until people learn to observe their own being and world history in light of karma (vol. 7, p. 95).

Memories and More

Consider the death of a friend, or father or mother: "Let's compare the full intensity of the event and the moment when it was experienced to the shadowy memories that come to us ten years later! And yet we must have those shadowy memories in order to be aware of the continuity, the intrinsic value and reality of our 'I,' in earthly life. But isn't it evident from this how the 'I'— which can find no bearings in earthly life without memory—really experiences itself in a shadowy way and how it is anchored in what actually sinks down every night into unconsciousness! As a matter of fact, we do not experience our 'I' with very great intensity in our ordinary level of consciousness on Earth. The real 'I' of life, which is not immediately present, grows increasingly akin to thought, although we know that it is connected with the "I" of today. Experience of the present has intensity, but this intensity is absent from experiences that have become memories.... The characteristic feature of this memory is that feeling, as well as impulses of will, are increasingly sifted out of it. However intense our feelings may have been on the occasions referred to—the death of someone extraordinarily dear to us, for instance—yet the memory picture that remains has become dim, increasingly devoid of feeling. And even less is there any continuance of what we then undertook through our will impulses under the impression of the moment! Feeling and will fade away; as a rule, the calm memory picture, a mere shadow of what we actually experienced, is all that remains" (vol. 7, p. 97).

> **Assignment:** Discuss this in relation to your experiences of loss. We experience memories very differently than we do present experiences. Is there a kind of "protection" in that as well? The shadow may be like the veils of mist on an early morning meadow.

Regarding thankfulness: "The most beautiful way for one's personality to be led into the suprasensory is when the path leads through thankfulness to life. Gratitude is also a way into the suprasensory, and it finally becomes veneration and love for the life-bestowing human spirit. Thankfulness gives birth to love, and when love is born from gratitude toward life, it opens the heart to the spiritual powers that permeate all existence" (vol. 7, p. 99).

We must have thankfulness to our birth and even before, to prenatal existence. We come to something that is mightier than our "I"—we approach the events and creative forces that directed us into life on Earth: "It is through this thankfulness and love that a presentiment of irrevocable destiny comes. When we have divined the existence of this ruling destiny, having experienced thankfulness and love, we begin to feel the power of the events that made us what we are" (vol. 7, p. 100).

Consider the example of a poet who would never have found his true vocation had he not failed his school examination at eighteen. If he had passed, he would have become an excellent financial inspector, but his true calling would never have come forth. Even events that seem to go "against us" help to forge our destiny!

A key to practicing the exercises in Steiner's book, *How to Know Higher Worlds*, is to look with composure and objectivity at the hard experiences of one's life. With Imagination and Inspiration, we can experience things with deeper significance and transform the experiences into pictures full of content.

"Deeper spiritual connections become evident, and a picture arises that is also carried about with us when the experience has passed. The experience has passed, but the picture is immediately present. The experience is intense and, through Imagination, the spiritual connections play into it. The soul is stirred strongly, and it is then possible to look into the spiritual reality and to retain the experience. If a night goes by, the experience—which has become more intense because the astral body and the 'I' go out of the physical body—is carried into the spiritual world. What has been experienced in the physical world with the physical and etheric bodies together can be experienced in the spiritual world with only the 'I' and astral body. On waking, however, it [that experience] is driven back into the physical body. But it is not brought back as if by the ordinary consciousness, which is restricted to memories that gradually fade away. It is carried back so that our whole being is permeated, as by a phantom; it is carried with us in full objectivity, in all intensity, and it resounds with the reality of another human being standing bodily before us.... The experiences are not alone; they are now colored by what produced them in former earthly lives, by the forecast of how they will go on working in the earthly lives to come... they become transparent as glass, and behind them, like a mighty cosmic memory, stands evolving karma, the objectivized memory. We become aware not only that human beings have within them the shadowy memories of earthly life, but also that our karma is engraved around us in the cosmic ether, the Akashic Chronicle. Within is shadowy memory; without is the cosmic memory of our destiny through our lives on Earth, although it remains unknown to our ordinary consciousness" (vol. 7, pp. 102–03).

> **Assignment:** Do an exercise with a past experience by carrying it over several nights and reflecting on how your inner relationship to it changes with time.

Steiner then sketches a person walking on the Earth, bearing a shadowy memory. Then comes a little cloud in the region of the head, an etheric aura in which the experiences are inscribed from the previous earthly life. We have an inner memory, and we have the world's memory outside us. "Every human being is surrounded by this aura. Not only is the present life engraved in us by way of memory, but earthly human lives, too, are engraved round about us. It is not always easy to decipher this memory, but it is there" (vol. 7, p. 103). We have a memory within and an auric memory around us! "This inkling of being enclosed in a karmic-auric mangle can come to us. It will take more than a period of a few days, as would be possible with Initiation knowledge, but it will come about gradually in the course of more intimate self-observation—often with respect to experiences lying in the far past to which we turn our gaze" (vol. 7, p. 104).

"Unfortunately, however, it is rare today for people to penetrate so deeply into their own souls that they achieve this grasp of their own experiences or even come close to developing a feeling of thankfulness. People today take life in a far too external way. They rush through life without pausing quietly to realize the nature of their various experiences" (vol. 7, p. 104).

> **Assignment:** How can we learn to pause for a while...*non fa niente* (Italian, "it doesn't matter") or *slappe* (Danish, "relax"), finding "sabbath" moments in everyday life? (Note: see Wayne Muller, *Sabbath: Finding Rest, Renewal, and Delight in Our Busy Lives*.)

Steiner offers examples of history teachers. One taught with enthusiasm and was popular, but then gradually lost it over the years. Another teacher was also excellent, but then changed jobs to become an administrative director, doing much more trivial work for the rest of his life. Why? Many people today take life superficially—sitting all day in cafés or playing billiards. Why? "In that previous incarnation, when they were already clever and intelligent, the culture of the age prevented them from knowing anything about the Earth's connection with spiritual life in the cosmos. Because they stumbled, as it were, through life—thinking of Earth as enclosed in itself with nothing but physical stars to be seen outside—in the next incarnation, they can turn to meet the impacts of real life only with stumbling steps.... But thoughts about karma must do more than introduce mere reflections into our life; they must bring *will* activity" (vol. 7, p. 109).

> **Assignment:** How can we do this?

Unit 47:
Sleep

Karmic Relationships, vol. 7, lecture 8

Sleep can give us hints regarding individual karma, especially about the difference between the two moments of waking up and going to sleep. "The moment of going to sleep is especially evident to people who are sick or ailing. They notice more readily than do those in good health that the moment of going to sleep is often accompanied by at least a slight feeling of pleasure. The moment of waking, however, has something slightly unpleasant about it. Waking is accompanied by happiness only when our attention is immediately turned toward the outer world and when our consciousness of the outer world drowns what is rising from within us. For many people, the moments of both waking and going to sleep are shrouded in a certain dimness. At the moment of going to sleep, we have the feeling that we are somehow dragging the day's experiences along with us—that they become increasingly nebulous and that we then abandon them. The moment of waking is accompanied by a slight feeling of oppression, a feeling of lifting oneself out of certain depths, bringing from them something that is carried over into the day and is gotten rid of only during the course of the day. The result is that a certain feeling of unpleasantness may be associated with the experience of waking. An unpleasant sensation of taste may intensify into an equally unpleasant sensation of a stupefied head" (vol. 7, p. 111).

Assignment: What have been your recent experiences of waking and sleeping?

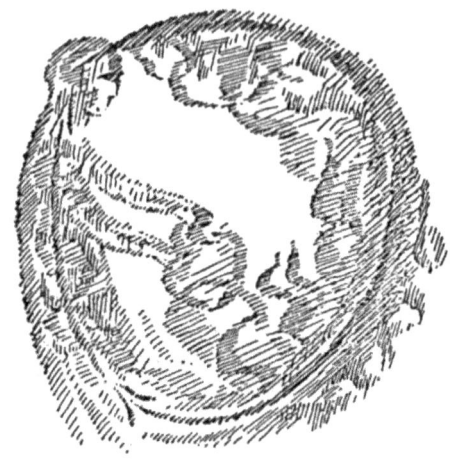

Drawing on page 112

"So, the waking hours of the day are used for the purpose of bringing our 'I' and astral body slowly into our physical and etheric bodies, from the tips of our fingers and toes" (vol. 7, p. 113).

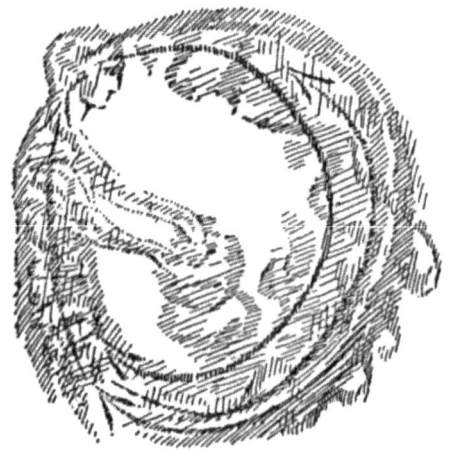

Drawing on page 114

Two currents stream toward each other: One is experienced especially on going to sleep, and the other is experienced vividly during the first decades after death, when life is relived in reverse order. If we were able to pass into sleep with full consciousness, we would live through the day's experiences in reverse order, but in pictures. During the first decade after death all this is experienced as a *reality*.

"When this second stream is fully perceptible to Initiation vision, it is seen to be a repository of the whole karmic past, which passes before a human being every time he sleeps. Whereas a person can experience something of the karma that is taking shape for the future, when he wakes from sleep, he has in the feeling I have described a faint, admittedly a very faint, glimpse of his present karma. The moment of waking brings a faint indication of what an individual bears inwardly from past earthly lives. This is, of course, taken into what the astral body and 'I' radiate when—from the tips of the fingers and toes—they spread through the body. A very burdensome karma, a karma that is difficult to bear, radiates unhealthy material deposits into the head, whereas a good karma radiates health-bringing deposits.... From bad karma, from the residue of whatever guilt has been incurred, unhealthy deposits in the human organism are reduced to a kind of vapor that rises into the head. The head then feels dull and heavy. The weaving of karma right into the physical can be perceived from the conditions prevailing on waking in the morning. Karma takes shape through the alternating effects of sleeping and waking life.... Thus, sleep is actually the window through which we look at our karma. We become familiar with this karma and work at its further formation during sleep through the deeds and thoughts that fill our waking life.

This is the first weaving of karma: it takes place during sleep. We have already considered a second weaving, which takes place during the first decades after death" (vol. 7, pp. 115–16).

> **Assignment:** Upon waking have you sometimes felt that experiences have been reviewed during the night and have now given you a new perspective? Can you share examples?

"We sink into sleep every night because it is then that we work at the formation of our karma, and because it is during sleep that our karma from previous earthly lives finds the way it can play a role in our daily life. From the night, karma gradually enters our daily life and we bring something quite definite with us into the day. Those who can recollect clearly how at one point in life a particularly significant event occurred to them will easily perceive—if they have a more intimate, finely developed faculty of introspection—that if such an event took place, let's say, in the afternoon, ever since morning an inner restlessness was impelling them toward it.... On days when something important is to happen to us, we do not wake up exactly as we do on days that take their usual course—but we do not notice it. Those who used to lead peasant lives on the land knew about these things and disliked being torn suddenly out of sleep, because without a gradual transition into the waking life of day we are wrested away from these intimate experiences. Peasants say that, on waking, we should never look at the window immediately but away from it so that, while the light is still dim, we can become aware of what is emerging from sleep" (vol. 7, pp. 116–17). Alarm clocks are not good for us!

When we dream about a person, it is often someone we knew in a past life. Those we meet and about whom we never dream were most likely not with us in a past incarnation. For example: "Now imagine that someone is living at the present time...having lived previously in the fourteenth or the eleventh century. During the life in the eleventh century, that individual performed a truly significant act, one that made a very strong impression on the astral body. The ensuing result remains in the astral body, and when that person comes again in the twentieth century it wants finally to be fulfilled and, from this astral body, to give the necessary stimulus. When the result of the experience in the eleventh century is of such significance that it cannot use a feeble, aged astral body, barely capable of performing important deeds, then it must use an astral body in the early years of life. And if the event has been so important as to eclipse all other events of life, a great deal must be compressed into the period while the astral body is still youthful. What does this mean? It means that the individual concerned will have a *short life* in the [current] incarnation. Here you see how the length of life is determined by the effects of former earthly thoughts and deeds being anchored in the astral body" (vol. 7, p. 119).

Evil deeds in one life can also make a strong impact on the astral body in the next: "...bad karma batters the organs, softens them, and causes disease. Now comes the second incarnation. Such actions or thinking in the eleventh century can inflate the astral body, thereby condemning the individual to death at an early age. But one may fall ill in any case, apart from this violent impact; a person might have a severe illness and die from it.... And the death sends the illness on in advance...we become ill so that we may die at the right moment.... That is the karmic aspect of illness. This karmic aspect of illness can be an extremely important factor for diagnosis" (vol. 7, p. 120).

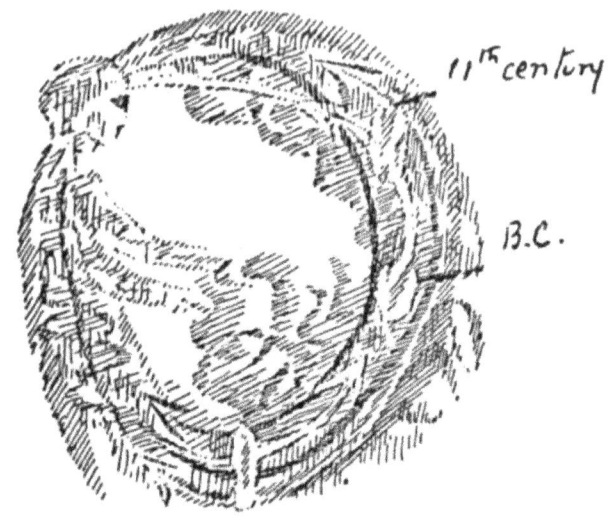

Drawing on page 121

"In the case of illness, therefore, when we see how far back the influential events lie, karma can indicate to us that an affliction of the legs, for example, arises from incarnations in the relatively recent past, whereas a symptom of illness in the head comes from incarnations in the relatively far distant past. Thus, the transition from the spiritual into the physical can also be indicated by karma" (vol. 7, p. 121).

This is important for therapy: "The remedy for illness affecting the head will be found in what existed very far back in the evolutionary process of nature, in what is reminiscent of very early nature processes—for instance, mushrooms, which in the present, imperfect form recapitulate an earlier plant formation, or in algae and lichens or, in the case of the fully developed plant, in the root, since that is the part that has remained at the earliest stage. Illness in the lower body and more toward its periphery will have to be healed with what appeared at a later stage in the evolution of nature—namely, blossoms, flowering plants, or also with later formations in the mineral kingdom. Whatever is a later development in human beings must be healed with what is also a late development in nature" (vol. 7, p. 122). "Nothing can lead more positively to realization of the spiritual than the study of karma" (vol. 7, p. 123).

"When we see again how the lives of individuals are shortened and they die at an early age—indicating that karma has inflated their astral body and must make strong demands upon it as the result of past deeds, thus contributing to illness—the working of karma is in evidence everywhere. Or let us suppose someone has an accident and is ill as a result; then, under certain circumstances, such an accident—which is possibly, but not necessarily, determined by karma—can continue to be a factor in the further course of karma through following lives on Earth. Illness may also be the *beginning* of karma, and then it will be found that such illnesses make going to sleep an unwelcome and difficult process. But when illnesses are the beginning of karma, there is something consoling about them...illnesses that are a fulfillment of karma and make waking unpleasant, point to previous experiences. Illnesses that are an augury of future karma and make going to sleep an unwelcome and difficult process are the beginning of good karma, for there will be compensation for what is suffered in such an illness. We have the pain now and afterward the compensation for the pain, the uplifting, joyous experience.... Sleeplessness can sometimes be a good comforter, and if it were not karmically beneficial in its spiritual aspect, it would be much more harmful than it actually is" (vol. 7, pp. 123–24).

UNIT 48:
THREEFOLD HUMANS

Karmic Relationships, vol. 7, lecture 9

"Our inner, moral impulses do not proceed from the head but from the region of the metabolic-limb system, not however, from the physical system but from its constitution of soul and spirit wherein thrones and cherubim and seraphim are living.... Here on Earth, human beings look upward, to the heavens in order to divine a higher reality, a spiritual suprasensory reality. We do this as long as we are on the Earth. If we are living between death and a new birth, we look downward and behold what the moral content of one's soul becomes as a result of the deeds of the cherubim, seraphim, and thrones. There, below, when we descend again to Earth, the consequences are fulfilled... we send the consequences of our deeds of the present into the next earthly life" (vol. 7, p. 129).

"The metabolic-limb system... works in karma [and] karma brings the head across from one earthly life into another. Thus, karma is active directly in the formation of the head. And if we begin to develop an unbiased view of humankind in this field, we will gradually learn to read a great deal about our karma from the physiognomy of the head. Every human being has one's own particular head; no single individual has exactly the same shaped head as another. Although individuals often look alike, they are not alike in their karma. In the head formation, the karma of one's past is revealed to physical sensory perception. In the metabolic-limb system lies *future* karma; spiritually concealed, it is there invisibly. So, if we speak of humankind in the spiritual sense we can say: Human beings are constituted so that, on the one hand, we make our past karma visible and, on the other hand, we bear our future karma invisibly within us" (vol. 7, p. 131).

> Assignment: Try a clay modeling exercise showing the morphology of limbs and head. (Note to reader: see L. F. C. Mees, *Secrets of the Skeleton: Form in Metamorphosis.*)

"The head is generally the most highly valued, but it is not the most perfect in a spiritual respect. For whereas thrones, cherubim, and seraphim live in the metabolic-limb system, in the head system live archai, archangeloi, angeloi. It is they who stand behind everything we experience with our head in the physical world of sense. They live in us, in our head system, and are active behind our consciousness; they encounter the effects of the physical world and mirror them back, and we become conscious only of the reflections" (vol. 7, p. 132). Between the nerves-sense system in the head and the metabolic system, we have a rhythmic system of lungs and heart, where the activity of the exousiai, dynamis, and kyriotetes lives.

Example of reincarnation (vol. 7, pp. 134–35): There was once a slave owner who had an overseer with responsibility to enforce harsh punishments on all who were enslaved on the plantation. The overseer did this reluctantly but was so enmeshed in the system, he felt he had no choice but to deal harshly with any infraction. In the next incarnation, they returned during the Middle Ages and became man and wife, living in a small village. The woman had been the overseer, and the slave owner was now the police jailor. For the most part, the villagers were reincarnations of the slaves who had been ill-treated by the former slave owner. He was now held responsible for all that happened in that village commune. However, because the wife shared in all the suffering that the one-time slaves caused her husband, "**the karma was fulfilled between her—the former overseer—and the slave owner**" (vol. 7, p. 135).

In the next incarnation, now in the nineteenth century, the former overseer returned as the great educational reformer, *Pestalozzi*, "**and those who had been the slaves under him were now the children who received such infinite benefit from his educational principles**" (vol. 7, p. 135).

> **Assignment:** Discuss the implications of this for teachers and parents. Who are the children who have become our students?

Unit 49:
Tintagel and More

Karmic Relationships, vol. 8, lectures 1–3

Rudolf Steiner offered this personal reflection: at an early age he could grasp and understand mathematics, wave theory, and so on, but he had great difficulty recognizing a mineral, even after he had seen it several times. **"I found it difficult to retain concrete pictures of the things of the external, material world. It was not easy for me to come fully into the physical world of sense"** (vol. 8, p. 14).

In earlier times, people saw cosmic intelligence as pervading everything. Intelligence was not thought to be a personal, individual thing but was seen as a gift of the gods. Human intelligence was considered a drop of universal intelligence, manifesting in the individual. Head and heart were integral parts of universal intelligence.

> **Assignment:** What are the implications of going from a threefold to twofold view of humans?

The rulership of archangels: At the time of Alexander the Great, Michael was the ruling archangel, followed by Oriphiel, and then Anael, Zachariel, Raphael, and Samael, each age lasting three to four centuries. Gabriel was regent from the fifteenth until the final third of the nineteenth century, when Michael resumed dominion. In all, seven archangels rule in succession.

As a result of incarnations of personalities mentioned and the meeting in the spiritual world of Alexander and Aristotle with Haroun al Rashid and his wise counselor, human beings descended into the sensory world, and a great longing for the spiritual worlds arose in subsequent incarnations. Many of these people have found their way into the Anthroposophical Society.

And many of those involved in anthroposophy at the time of Steiner found their way back to Earth sooner than usual—at the turn of the twentieth to twenty-first century. The very understanding of these spiritual impulses has given us the impulse to return and continue work during the age of Michael. Thus **"your membership in this movement is deeply connected with your karma"** (vol. 8, p. 30).

Thomas Aquinas
Illustration on page 34:
Thoughts radiating down from cosmic intelligence.

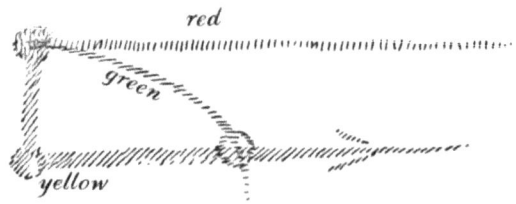

Illustration on page 35:
Thoughts became increasingly Earth-centered over time.

"An example of how in earlier times people sought cosmic intelligence in a way that it is no longer sought today can to be found when one stands, as we were able to do last Sunday, at the place in Tintagel that was once the site of King Arthur's castle and where he with his twelve companions exercised a power of far-reaching significance for Europe" (vol. 8, p. 39). King Arthur and the Round Table of twelve formed a Michaelic community representing the stage when Archangel Michael still administered cosmic intelligence. "At the ruins of King Arthur's castle today, the akasha chronicle still preserves the picture of the stones falling from those once-mighty gates, and those falling stones become an image of the cosmic intelligence falling, sinking away from the hands of Michael into human minds and hearts" (vol. 8, p. 38). This is in opposition to Parsifal and the Grail, where thoughts find their way to the "pure fool," and thoughts now need to be found within the earthly sphere.

Two streams—the Arthurian stream and the Grail stream. The great problems for humanity:

1. How can the Michael rulership bring about a deeper understanding of Christianity?
2. Within the Grail stream, how can the Christ impulse take expression in a different way, now as part of Earth?

"The spiritual Essence of the Sun is now united with earthly evolution—such was the conviction" (vol. 8, p. 41). The School of Chartres stands midway between the Arthurian principle in the north and the Grail principle in the south.

Unit 50:
Elementals, Karma, and Indigenous Wisdom

Karmic Relationships, vol. 8, lecture 4

In ancient times, human beings could look at trees, animals, mountains, and rocks and feel that they were living with spirit beings and human souls who were not presently incarnated on the Earth. "Spirit beings made their way into physical habitations as though into their homes. No wonder that all these things passed over into the myths and then people spoke of tree spirits, water spirits, spirits of clouds and mountains, for they saw companions of the night disappearing into the mountains, into the waves, into the clouds, and into the plants and trees" (vol. 8, p. 48).

Levels of consciousness began to change with time:

Waking consciousness—fading astral vision
Dream consciousness—fading vision of the spiritual world
Sleep consciousness—fading vision of karma

Over 10,000 years or more, great changes took place in human beings: "Humankind 'wakes' away—not only 'sleeps' away—the spiritual reality in the physical world. People 'wake' away the spiritual in nature and 'dream' away the true spiritual world. People 'sleep' away their karma" (vol. 8, p. 51). We gain a new freedom, but our heightened earthly wakefulness has come at a price.

Today, "by accepting the new initiation science, we must learn in our present-day consciousness to recognize the spirit and as we look at every rock or tree or cloud or star or Sun or Moon, to recognize the spiritual beings in all their diversity" (vol. 8, p. 52).

> Assignment: Have you experienced "waking, dreaming, sleep consciousness" at different geographic locations and with various cultures on this Earth?

"In the future, we can gradually reclaim the faculty to see tree spirits come forth from the trees...and we will also once again be able then to see people who approach us with heightened perception—the ability to see emerge from them the figures of earlier lives together with the evolution of their karma. For this kind of vision leads on to a vision of karma" (vol. 8, p. 54).

Mineral world—dwarfs, then vision of seraphim, cherabim, thrones
Plant world—exusiai, dynamis, kyriotetes
Animal world—archai, archangels, angels
Human kingdom—this vision leads to karma

"For, behind all the mysteries of the world lies, in truth, the great mystery of human karma" (vol. 8, p. 55). Here, Steiner demonstrates his grasp of what we can find in Indigenous cultures.

> Assignment: Find a story or example from an indigenous culture in which we can see the spirit working. If possible, participate in a nature-drawing workshop to strengthen your perception of nature.

Unit 51:
History through Biography

Karmic Relationships, vol. 8, lectures 5 and 6

Much of history remains unexplained when using conventional methods: "The truth is that the events in human history become comprehensible only when we look at the personalities who play a decisive part in these events, in respect of their repeated lives on Earth" (vol. 8, p. 56). This is because things that happen in history are enacted by people who have brought over intentions from earlier epochs. Thus, we need to look at external events against the background of human destinies. A holistic view of history!

> **Assignment:** Look for things that are inexplicable in history, things that make you wonder why. Then do a study of some of the key players involved. Each person can take one historical figure and research the biography.

Thus, we need to look at the *whole human being* and not just what is visible at first glance. Examples:

1. Steiner's Geometry teacher with a club foot: Karmic law: "What was head organization in the previous life becomes foot or limb organization, and what had been the foot or limb organization becomes head organization" in the next life.

2. Lord Byron, lecturer who always blew his nose before speaking: little characteristic actions of a person, such as the way one moves the fingers, can lead the way to karmic connections far more quickly than any outstanding activities one may have taken.
3. Voltaire—influenced by the Mars stage of life between death and rebirth.
4. Ignatius Loyola—his karmic experiences brought him into the vicinity of Mars beings. Wounded leg. Jesuit Order and unconditional obedience to the Pope. "A great selflessness that is present in Jesuitism and again signifies a tremendous increase of strength, for everything a person does with intense energy, putting forth all of one's force and acting not on one's own authority nor out of emotion—everything a person does in this way gives extraordinary strength to one" (vol. 8, p. 66). "Loyola was able thereby to establish a retrospective connection as it were with those who came after him in the Jesuit order. He remained united with his order in the retrospect of his own life" (p. 67). And relatively soon after his earthly life was over, he reappeared in the soul of Emmanuel Swedenborg.

> **Assignment:** Journal and/or discuss how selflessness leads to strength.

> Learn to be silent and yours will be power.
> Forego the power and yours will be willing.
> Forego the willing and yours will be feeling.
> Forego the feeling and yours will be knowing.
> (Torin Finser, *Initiative*, p. 36)

Through the Mercury beings, illnesses are transformed into spiritual qualities. Thus, investigations into karma are often aided by looking at a person's connections to a disease (see *Extending Practical Medicine* by Rudolf Steiner and Ita Wegman).

The interplay of sun and waves, light and air, as seen from Tintagel by the Arthurian knights evoked a sense of *piety* as a result of the nature spirits. This poured into their hearts through their etheric bodies. **"They received into themselves the Christ impulse, which was then streaming away from the Sun and living in everything brought into being by the Sun forces"** (vol. 8, p. 77). Thus, Christ could influence people in pre-Christian, pagan times. It purified their astral forces so that the Arthurian knights could then go out into Europe with these purifying forces. **"The Mystery of Golgotha was revealed to them because the picture was all irradiated by the life spirit of Christ presented to them by nature"** (p. 79).

Two streams came to meet each other:

> Pre-Christian Christ in the etheric—Arthurian stream
> After Mystery of Golgotha—Grail stream

The spiritual etheric *Image* of the Christ came from the West, and the Christ being himself came from the East. The two met in Europe during the ninth century.

A clarion call for working with Anthroposophy in this time of crisis: **"Human beings today are facing a great crisis. Either they must see civilization going down into the abyss, or they must raise it through spirituality and promote it in the sense of the Michael impulse"** (vol. 8, p. 93).

> **Assignment:** What are the implications for the current time in which we live?

Appendix

Unless otherwise noted, the following articles are by Torin M. Finser and are included to deepen some of the aspects covered in the fifty-two units.

Our Karmic Companions

Think back to a time when you went on a trip with friends, perhaps a multi-day hike, a visit to Mexico, or a retreat or training program. By the end of the experience there was a level of familiarity with the other participants that was not there at the beginning. You may not "like" everyone equally, some you may have even learned to avoid but, overall, there is often a feeling of warmth and camaraderie at the end of the trip or event. You know each other out of shared experiences, and in many cases, friendship has arisen. These new friends will henceforth be in your life, often despite miles of separation in the years to come. When you take up a conversation again, it will be like picking up the thread rather than beginning anew. On the trip or retreat you built a foundation of shared experience, you "bonded" and that has now become a wonderful new reality in your life.

This common experience gives one a taste of a larger version of bonding we can call karma and reincarnation. One may not be at first comfortable with the idea, but, if one can entertain some of the aspects I plan to introduce, it can prove helpful to administrators and leaders in the workplace. For karma is a longer version of the multi-day hike on the Appalachian trail, it is a journey over several lifetimes. Along the way one makes connections that carry over into subsequent lives, and their influence can be felt and experienced especially when one is in a close working situation with others.

It is one of the pleasures and challenges of working in a Waldorf school that one is united with others who share similar values. You are drawn by a mutual attraction to the mission and vision of the school, the philosophy and way of working with children. People find each other in common purpose and intention, and those who have been drawn together more often than not have connections that go far back.

This might not be visible at first, because after all each family is different, our children have different needs and some of us as parents may spend just a few minutes a day at the school. But the more involved we become, and especially if one takes up work with real responsibilities at the school, the connections tend to surface more readily. At first it may be a matter of mutual interest: "oh, you love good jazz, too," or, "yes, I have always had an herb garden." When these mutual interests become known it is like fireflies lighting up the night. The many points of discovery bring great joy. We realize the school is not just for our children, but we too have many wonderful reasons to associate with the other families.

These connections can intensify over time, to the point at which some of the other adults at the school become your best friends. These are the people you invite to a family celebration; these are the ones you choose to take to a concert or a local restaurant. These friendships can become so strong that they endure even after the children have graduated.

But even on the friendship level some complexity can arise. What if you are a parent who is asked to serve on the board of trustees and one of your best friends is the board president?

Roles have a way of changing, and there may be times when you see things differently than your friend on the board. Or you may be a faculty member who is asked to serve a term on the board, and suddenly the relationship with some of your "friends" changes due to positions you take on certain issues. In most cases, these things can be worked through with good conversation and dialogue, but one needs to attend to the dynamic of changing roles.

When patterns of interaction emerge, either positive or negative ones, one often has a first glimpse of a larger dynamic (perhaps karma) at work. By patterns I mean things such as repeated outcomes of discussions in which two members are often on the same "side" or opposed to each other, even though the issue may be different each time. Behaviors, especially those that are more instinctive, show a connection to the will forces in the human being. And the will is a cosmic thread that connects our lives on earth. Briefly stated, when we die, we soon discard all our clever thoughts and gradually even our feelings leave the soul. But as the journey of life after death unfolds, the will forces that a person had in life are carried forward. In many cases we "will ourselves" into a new birth situation so that we have an opportunity to take on tasks that will assist us in our further development. We come back to earth with intentionality, with the wish to do more self-development and work especially with those people where there were unresolved tasks. We seek out the people we need to work with!

Opportunities

We often find many of our karmic companions in and around a Waldorf school. This can be a joyous discovery. Here are people for whom I feel great kinship! We quickly become friends, and we have so much fun together, we enjoy doing things together. When this happens with a whole group of people, one forms a kind of karmic cluster, like minded people who have much in common, much of it coming as a kind of "grace" that was not expected. Of course, some friendships one really has to work for, but our karmic companions are often thrust into our lives as if by an external force.

This affords us many opportunities. Countless Waldorf schools and other ventures have been started by karmic companions. There is no end to what these folks can do: construct buildings, fundraise, countless potlucks, recruit new families and teachers...the list goes on and on. Because of this familiar ground of friendship, much simply happens. At these early stages one does not need policies or procedures (or so it seems for a while) and people simply act out of trust and knowing each other. There is strength and vitality to working with karmic companions. So much can be accomplished.

These karmic groups often continue on long into the biography of a school. Sometimes the original founders change roles, some become teachers, others stay connected with the board, but for them the school was about more than educating children. It was a social opportunity to find one another again.

This last statement points to a highly potent spiritual force. We think we are the ones who "build" our schools, teach and administer them in the years that follow. But in fact we are but a small piece of the cosmic action. The finding of karmic companions unleashes tremendous creative forces in the world around us, like the Titans of ancient Greece, beings that use our activity as an opportunity to lend themselves to

Appendix: Our Karmic Companions

our intentions. Schools are built spiritually, not just physically. When we find our karmic companions and we pull together we are sending forth a mighty invitation to the spiritual worlds to invest in our endeavors. Especially in the age of Michael, this dynamic of human and cosmic collaboration is an ever-present reality for schools and other organizations founded on a spiritual view of the human being. We and our karmic companions do the inviting; the children and their friends respond on a physical level. The cosmos responds with unexpected resources and support that makes the impossible possible.

Challenges

Finding our karmic companions also presents challenges. We bring with us unresolved issues and even conflicts from the past. The school now becomes our opportunity to either resolve things or perpetuate them. In my experience, it is often some of both.

Rudolf Steiner gives us one example of this in a lecture given on February 20, 1912:

> So, the acquaintances we make somewhere around the age of thirty in one incarnation may have been, or will be, persons related to us by blood in a previous or subsequent incarnation. It is therefore useful to say to oneself: The personalities with whom life brings you in contact in your thirties were once around you as parents or brothers and sisters or you can anticipate that in one of your next incarnations, they will have this relationship with you. The reverse also holds true. (Steiner, *Reincarnation and Karma*, p. 56)

Thus, some of our karmic companions we find in a school may have been our siblings or parents in a past life, or the people we work with closely in the years of mid life may become blood ties in the next life. This sheds a whole new light on colleagueship. Just as with family members and deep connections, much is unspoken—so, too, with karmic companions in a school setting. We can also find a kind of sibling rivalry that seems unexplainable in terms of the flow of an average agenda. Why does so and so always seem to counter what she says in a meeting? These kinds of instinctive responses often point to deep pools of karma.

There is also a phenomenon I have long called a "karmic knot," such as a couple of people get so tied up in conflict there seems to be no end. Just as a knot becomes more difficult to untie when it is soaked in water and repeatedly dried, similarly with multiple earth lives there are karmic knots that a school simply cannot be untied in one generation. I have seen a teacher in such a karmic knot finally leave and do very well at another school. It is a deeply humbling experience to realize that not everything can be resolved in the present. Time is a great healer, and we often fail to use it wisely.

The negative side of karmic companionship is that the administration of the school can at times be held hostage to one or two well placed karmic knots. When this happens, progress is impeded and people start to walk in circles around the problem. One has to make every attempt to resolve an issue, and much can be resolved when given a healthy process and facilitation. Once it is resolved, all concerned reach a new level of working together that is no longer instinctive but born out of the trials of fire and water. The best antidote to the negative working of karma is hard-earned consciousness.

When we are aware of our own role in a situation and are able to see the larger dimensions of biography and karma at work, then the knots of life begin to relax. Sometimes one can go only so far and then has to decide: Can I now live with the situation? Has the healing gone far enough, or do I need to express my gratitude for the learning made possible in these circumstances and move on?

Speaking of moving on, I used to think that leaving a school is a sign of failure. But as with many things in life, my views have evolved. Of course, there is great value in perseverance and continuity, and many of our schools would not be where they are if some karmic companions had not stuck to it over time. For others, however, moving on can become a fresh start, a new beginning. Schools need new blood, new human impulses, and moving to another school can promote a "beginners mind" for the teacher, parent, or board member. Perhaps there are also other karmic companions waiting to meet us! Movement, as in nature, tends to promote life, and it is better to go with life than to stagnate.

And, of course, it is possible to enhance movement while staying with the same job; changing roles is one instance. I have done that several times while at Antioch University. One can strive to become a different person and bring inner movement to refresh and enliven outer circumstances. But, of course, that depends on the free resolve of those involved.

Postscript

I shared this short chapter with my father, Siegfried Finser, as he has spent many years living with and studying karma. He sent the following response, which I am permitted to include here:

An executive at Microsoft who had his children in the Seattle Waldorf School asked me, "What good is it to know about karma? How does it help me lead my life?" He and I worked together on his question. We realized that karma cannot be used as a guide to behavior or decision making. It can be useful only in deepening our understanding, enriching our awareness, and enlightening our empathy. Every time someone explains their behavior by saying they have a karmic relationship, it is a red flag, a kind of untruth. The only explanation for one's actual decisions or behaviors that holds water in our time is the self-directed, truthful reason for the action. Karma is part of the "world of necessity" that meets us out of the unknown. What we do should no longer be part of that. What we do should more and more be done out of the realm of freedom, our spiritual activity.

I myself am almost always aware of the karmic overtones and undertones. It's like the piano accompaniment to one's personal melody. I try to act having the awareness but not using it as a motive or reason for decisions. It is far too complicated for such simple application, hence R. Steiner's six volumes, which barely scratch the surface.

Threefold Human Nature and World Karma

We relate to the world differently depending on whether we are connecting through thinking, feeling or willing:

Thinking

Our thoughts truly live when in the spiritual worlds between a death and a birth. Once we come to the Earth, they are more like a shell, a corpse, of what they once were. Particularly since AD 333, our thoughts have become dead in an earthly context. Although this has made it possible for humans to exercise greater and greater freedom, we are often dealing in mere shadow forms of what once lived as living thinking. People of the East and those living in early times experience that a god lives in every thought; thoughts were connected to the divine.

Even today, when we think, we are able to connect with other people's thoughts and find a kind of universality. Insofar as we strive to understand and exercise true thinking (as free as possible of feeling and willing), we are the same throughout the world. We are most conscious of ourselves and others in thinking, and the striving human being can make great progress in self-knowledge.

Feeling

With feeling, we live in a semiconscious state of being. Thus, it is harder to achieve clarity as feelings ebb and flow within the soul. Yet we are often convinced that our own way of feeling is the right one. We have to exercise great effort to look into our own soul to find our true feelings and thus practice self-knowledge. Nevertheless, we must do this if we want to be honest with ourselves and truly "own" our feelings.

With our feelings, we are connected to one region of the world or another. We belong to a group or nationality within which we can experience affinity. It is world karma that we experience ourselves as a part of one family, clan, class, or nation. Our sense of connection to one or another group of people and a certain geographic location is a feeling connection. We recognize others and connect with them partly because of where they come from and our feeling response.

Willing

In our willing, we are deep in unconsciousness. Our will lives in the unconscious sphere of life, where we live the karmic pathways that give us direction. Every step we take, most of our actions, and many of the people we meet are the results of the stream of karma that lives in the unconscious. Karma leads us to most of the important points in life—to the decisive moments, both of certainty and of doubt. Preceding lives live on in us through our will.

Whereas we find the universal in humans through our thinking and our membership in a group through feeling, it is our will that reveals the particular individuality of a human being. In our will we are truly individual.

Thus, a key question for reflection and ongoing work is: How should we relate to others on this Earth? Do we choose to meet in the clarity of conscious thinking, in the "connectedness" of feeling, or in the deep karmic stream of willing? What is called for in a particular situation? How can we best serve others in this project we can call world karma? What does it mean to see the phenomena and respond as a thinking, feeling, or willing human being? What is needed from us?

"Thy Will Be Done, on Earth as It Is in Heaven..."

These lines from the well-known prayer have for some time given me a source of contemplation. How do these words speak to us? Recently, I considered them from the vantage point of reincarnation and karma. "Thy will" most clearly refers to the will of God. What does it mean to have the same "will" at work on the Earth as it is in the heavens? Is the earthly realm a replication of the spiritual worlds? Does this form a kind of necessity?

There is much in Rudolf Steiner's karma studies that speaks to an enactment on Earth of what has been prepared in the journey between death and rebirth. Does "Thy will" work through all of these stages as well? Does it work even through the evil and the struggles that follow on Earth?

In Steiner's karma lectures, there are many descriptions of what could be called the cosmic mirror. After death, we see our actions from the past life through the "eyes" of the others with whom we lived on Earth—their experiences of our actions and words are reflected back to us. In this way, "Earth" is mirrored back to us in "Heaven." Then, in the next life, we place ourselves in situations according to what we have learned in the spiritual worlds; our intentions in "Heaven" are then reflected back to us on "Earth."

What is God's will? Many world religions view this as coming from single deity, the One above all. That is the reality for many. Could it also be that "God's will" is also the expression of all the spiritual processes, including those involving karma and reincarnation, that weave the tapestry we call life? And might our companion in that weaving of life's tapestry be called the Christ?

Karmic Leadership

In the context of current events in 2025, our collective images of leadership are perhaps more conflicted than ever. Yet this situation can provide an opportunity for Waldorf schools and other service-oriented nonprofit organizations to model alternative examples. At a time when the old forms of governance and past structures are being dismembered, Waldorf schools have a unique chance to stand for transformative leadership that inspires confidence and builds trust within the community.

Historically, leaders have been known as pharaohs, emperors, monarchs, generals, and politicians, most of whom ruled in hierarchical, top-down structures that perpetuated power dynamics until internal fissures (or the discontent of the masses) caused a collapse. The rise of democracy has provided an alternative, yet many aspects of an aristocratic world order still persist worldwide—even in our schools.

Many of the early Waldorf schools in North America were founded and led by singular, inspired leaders, who often presided for decades—Beulah Emmet at High Mowing School, Henry Barnes at Rudolf Steiner School in New York, and John Gardner at The Waldorf School of Garden City. The decades following their departure often witnessed a more collective, faculty-centered approach, sometimes chaotic in terms of administrative functioning, which often led to hiring school administrators and individuals with skill-based expertise, although many lacked any background in Waldorf, let alone anthroposophy. Most recently, we have seen the appointment of heads of school, pedagogical directors, and lead administrators. When things are going well, many organizations expand the circle of responsibility, whereas in times of crisis or financial pressure schools tend to go vertical again. Compliance issues in public Waldorf schools or the preferences of board members often push schools toward efficiency and increased hierarchy, while shared interest in students, curriculum development, and parent-teacher relationships tend to foster community. These creative tensions ebb and flow, but repeating patterns raise the question: Are we willing to reexamine assumptions about leadership and take some risks by moving beyond survival mode to tapping new resources spiritually and organizationally? It might help if we look more deeply at what happens when schools bring people together.

Leaders as Karmic Facilitators

We know leaders facilitate meetings—sometimes far too many each week! Navigating the ship of "school" through calm or turbulent waters is at times overwhelming. "I have no more bandwidth" is a phrase I hear more often these days. Another leader remarked recently that she has had to facilitate more interpersonal issues than ever before. What is going on? Is this due to post-Covid aftershocks? Loss of listening skills or diminished empathy for others? There might be many valid responses, but with the passage of time I have become less satisfied with the presenting issues and more intent on finding the deeper causes of organizational dysfunction and leadership fatigue. This search has led me to ask: Are Waldorf schools karmic communities?

Upon reflection, this question has been part of my life for a long time—as a class teacher working with colleagues, parents, and students; as an adult educator working with future teachers; and, especially, when trying to support school leaders who often work with exceptionally challenging situations. In this brief article I would like to present a few preliminary considerations, from the perspective of Waldorf schools, as opportunities for karmic reconciliation, particularly from a leadership perspective:

1. Given the journey between death and a new birth, the encounters along the way, and resolutions made as a result, many of us come into a new life on earth with intentions to seek out those with whom we have karmic connections.
2. We tend to reincarnate with these kindred souls again and again.
3. Especially during the first 21 years of life, we are faced with karmic obligations. We are born into a certain family constellation at a particular location on the Earth. We encounter people in school communities with whom we have unfinished work. There is an element of equality in this shared experience because we share so many obligations with those with whom we have previously lived.
4. Once we have accomplished some work with these "obligations," we enter a period of karmic fulfillment during our years 28 to 49 and beyond. During these years, many parents and teachers have children and find one another in Waldorf school communities. Karmic connections come to meet us face to face—literally! The key to success in these middle years depends on the transformative work that is available in human relationships. This striving develops empathy (for self and others) and the possibility for establishing a new sister-/brotherhood in community. Despite the challenges (and traveling many circuitous ways to get

there), many people feel inwardly fulfilled by having found kindred spirits in a Waldorf setting.
5. Then, during the years 56 to 77, we can enter the phase of free karmic sacrifice. If we have worked spiritually on ourselves, we can move more readily beyond the boundaries of our personal self and allow liberated soul forces to flow into the social life. This is possible because, during the years after 56, the human spiritual life increasingly separates from the physical life. As we age, we can be filled increasingly with the spirit, receiving direct nourishment from the cosmic hierarchies. In this period of karmic sacrifice, we can become, in freedom, servants of the world.

Today, more than ever, we need to find the forces to transform karmic obligations that we brought with us from our prenatal life into karmic fulfillment in our present life. This can give us the capacity for free karmic sacrifices in later years. Likewise, by embracing stages that in succession foster equality, sister-/brotherhood, and then freedom, we have an opportunity to realize aspects of the threefolding of social architecture, part of the often silent "promise" of engagement in Waldorf schools.

From a leadership perspective, rather than just seeking to put out "brush fires" and "fix" the issue du jour, we need to adopt the attitude of a midwife or facilitator—How can I help you realize your karmic intentions in this situation? What is seeking to find "birth" here? This gesture is needed not only with "victims" but also with "perpetrators" in disputes. Instead of merely placating enough to move on (the frequent "management" perspective in administration), the inner gesture of a leader can rise to a level of karmic facilitation. This happens when we start to inwardly carry the frequently unspoken karmic burdens of others (as well as our own). If we truly wish to realize community, we each need to carry something of the other person's karmic obligation to facilitate fulfillment in community.

Rudolf Steiner gave a number of specific karmic exercises to help us develop our capacity to work with the riddles of life. For several years now, I have included them in all of our Center for Anthroposophy leadership development residencies. Some exercises work immediately, others, such as the three-night exercise, require much patience. But I am convinced that leaders can no longer see karma studies as a subject just for anthroposophic study groups. In fact, thanks to the Michaelic nature of our present-day tasks in Waldorf communities, we need to work, consciously and intentionally, through what Steiner called "relics of old karma." We have a particularly diverse assortment of such karmic relics in our schools, and we ignore them at our peril. In fact, Steiner further indicates that, if we do not engage them, we will be hindered increasingly from doing our work in everyday life. Ordinary tasks (indeed, more and more of the "presenting issues") will take longer to resolve so long as we avoid the underlying spiritual causes.

When we have leaders who are willing to take courage in hand and facilitate karmic encounters, everyone can attain new freedom. And with the new freedom granted to us, we can find what we are really meant to do, in our school communities and as individuals. Is it possible to lift our gaze and accomplish tasks with new insight and, ultimately, practice free karmic sacrifice? This means giving to others out of recognition of who they are striving inwardly to become, not just through what we observe outwardly. Rather than facilitating only meetings, leaders can also help to birth new capacities. Under these conditions, there are truly no limits to the potential success of our Waldorf school communities. Since the spirit is magnificently potent, working with our anthroposophic foundations can enhance resilience. Such vibrancy can manifest outwardly in greater recognition, enrollment, funding, and future teachers and school leaders.

Our children are far closer to perfect than are many other humans on the planet today. Those who consider themselves adults (teachers, administrators, and parents) have an obligation to overcome their karmic relics in the spirit of service; they need to become new again, to be worthy of the confidence shown by the spiritual worlds when gifted with children to teach, love, and protect. Our servant leaders are also our karmic guardians.*

---

* This article by Torin Finser originally appeared in the fall 2025 issue of *School Renewal Magazine*, a biannual publication of AWSNA (www.waldorfeducation.org/waldorf-school-renewal-magazine/).

On Karma
Steffen Hartmann

Four-day Karmic Exercise

Key question: "How can I arrive at authentic karmic-knowledge judgments? To make matters worse, the adversarial powers know about human karma and want to use this knowledge to manipulate and interfere with it. Confusion and errors in the field of karmic knowledge—in addition to pure illusions—are caused by individuals recognizing karma either too early or too late. This creates disorder in karma and in the karmic connections between people" (pp. 3–5).

We need specific karmic exercises and practices to overcome this. A four-day exercise is one such example.

Steiner Spoke of "Putting Karma in Order"

Johannes Greiner: "Usually, the greatest obstacle to present-day work consists in the habits arising out of a past life. To recognize and transform one's own shadow is far more important than to point out errors of perception in other striving people!" (p. 14).

Anton Kimpfler: "At a certain point where we develop our own powers, our esoteric efforts become unfruitful if we do not enter the social sphere with them. Only when we learn to pass on the powers we have acquired will they remain good" (p. 16).

We Need to Work with Unredeemed Karmic Patterns

The veil that unconsciously separates us from the spiritual Michael school, into which we dive every night during sleep, has become even thinner and more transparent than before. This presents a great opportunity! Michael is closer than ever. However, he leaves us free, waiting upon our initiative (p. 18).

Appendix: On Karma

The Michaelic power of discernment characterized here necessitates that we pass through the individual karmic eye of the needle, and not once, but repeatedly. In the presence of Michael, knowledge and life, thinking and will are inseparable. The eye of the needle must be traversed in order to achieve a new sun-like quality. This shines in a creative way and gives us new courage for the future (p. 18).

Kaspar Hauser and the Purity of His Unspoiled Sensory Experience (Pure Perception)

Ahriman hates karma; Michael wants karma to be revealed; Christ can help us heal karma. Seven stages of karmic learning (p. 23; see pp 24–27 for detailed descriptions of each stage):

1. Emotional-memories
2. Dreams
3. Spontaneous imaginative memories
4. External events
5. Meditatively acquired memories/imaginations
6. Inspirational insights
7. Karmic intuitions

Overall process one of meditatively asking a karmic question and letting each step work so that one can unite with the stream of will of destiny.

Karmic work engages spirit remembrance ("Foundation Stone Meditation"). "Michael's pupils have to find and recognize one another in the earthly world" (p. 28).*

---

* From Steffen Hartmann, *The Michael Prophecy and the Years 2012–2033: Rudolf Steiner and the Culmination of Anthroposophy* (used by kind permission of Rudolf Steiner Press, Forest Row, UK).

Illness and Karma
Rudolf Steiner

You experience objectively in the spiritual world everything you yourself did in the external world, and in the process, you acquire the strength and the inclination to compensate for the pain in one of your future incarnations. Your own astral body tells you what it felt like, and you realize you have laid an obstacle in the way of your further development. This has to be cleared away, otherwise you cannot get beyond it. This is the moment you form the intention of getting rid of the obstacle. So, when you have lived through the Kamaloca period, you arrive back in your childhood filled with the intention of getting rid of all the hindrances you created in life. You are full of intentions, and it is the force of these intentions that brings about the special character of your future lives on earth.

Let us suppose that in his twentieth year B hurt A. He now has to feel the pain himself, and resolves to recompense A in a future life, that is, in the physical world, where the injury was done. The force of this good resolution forms a bond of attraction between B and A and brings them together in the next life. That mysterious force of attraction that brings people together in life springs from what they have acquired in Kamaloca. Our experiences there lead us to those people in life whom we have to recompense or with whom we have any kind of connection.

Now you will realize that the Kamaloca forces we have taken into ourselves for the righting of wrongs in life can by no means always be worked out in a single life. It can then happen that we form connections with a great number of

Appendix: Illness and Karma

people in one life, and that next time we are in Kamaloca we have the possibility of meeting them again. Now this depends, too, on the other people, whether we meet them again in the following life. That spreads itself over many lives. In one life we correct this, in another life that, and so on. You must certainly not imagine that we can immediately put everything right in one life. It depends entirely on whether the other person also develops in his soul the corresponding bond of attraction.*

After death, in looking back over life, we see what we have done wrong or otherwise; and, at the same time, we see how these deeds have affected ourselves; we see how, by a certain action, our characters have been improved or debased. If we have brought suffering to anyone, we have sunk and become of less value; we are less perfect, so to speak. Now, if we look back after death we see numerous events of the sort, and we say to ourselves: "I have deteriorated." Then in the consciousness after death, the will and power arise to win back, when the opportunities occur, the value we have lost; the will, that is to say, to compensate for every wrong committed. Thus, between death and rebirth, the tendency and intention are formed to make good what has been done wrong, in order to regain the standard of perfection a human being should have—a standard which has been lowered by the deed mentioned.**

---

* From Rudolf Steiner, *The Being of Man and His Future Evolution*, lecture 6: Illness and Karma, by Rudolf Steiner. Berlin. January 26, 1909.
** From Rudolf Steiner, *Manifestations of Karma*, p. 19 (1984 edition).

The Modern Human Being
Rudolf Steiner

The modern human being who has come into life at this time has stored up far too much karma not to feel connected by destiny with all whom one encounters in life. If we look back to previous ages, when souls were younger, we see that they had fewer karmic connections. Now it is simply a matter of necessity that we are awakened not only by nature but also by those human beings with whom we are karmically connected and whom we seek out.*

> Behold the Sun
> At the midnight hour!
> In the lifeless ground
> Build your rocky bower!
> So, when in depths you mourn,
> Find you in Death's dark night
> Creation's pulse newborn
> With living Morning Light.
> The Powers on high make known
> The eternal Word Divine;
> The Deeps must guard their own—
> Peace, in their sacred shrine.
> In gloom you live—
> Create anew a Sun!
> In matter weave—
> Know Spirit-bliss begun!**

---

* Rudolf Steiner, *Awakening to Community,* March 3, 1923.
** Verse by Rudolf Steiner, spoken by Marie von Sivers, Dec. 17, 1906.

Bibliography

Archiati, Pietro. *Reincarnation in Modern Life.* London: Temple Lodge, 1997.

Erdmann, Jens. *Wie Wirkt Es Wirklich?: Ein kleines Buch zu einer großen Frage.* Norderstedt, Germany: Books on Demand, 2022.

Finser, Torin M. *Education for Nonviolence: The Waldorf Way.* Great Barrington, MA: SteinerBooks, 2017.

———. *The False Door between Life and Death: Supporting Grieving Students, Teachers, and Parents.* Great Barrington, MA: SteinerBooks, 2019.

———. *Guided Self-study: Rudolf Steiner's Path of Spiritual Development: A Spiritual-Scientific Workbook.* Great Barrington, MA: SteinerBooks, 2015.

———. *In Search of Ethical Leadership: If not Now, When?* Great Barrington, MA: SteinerBooks, 2003.

———. *Initiative: A Rosicrucian Path of Leadership.* Great Barrington, MA: SteinerBooks, 2011.

———. *Leadership Development: Change from the Inside Out.* Great Barrington, MA: SteinerBooks, 2014.

———. *Listening to Our Teachers: Advocacy through Research.* Spencertown, NY: SteinerBooks, 2024.

———. *Organizational Integrity: How to Apply the Wisdom of the Body to Develop Healthy Organizations.* Great Barrington, MA: SteinerBooks, 2007.

———. *Parables.* Great Barrington, MA: SteinerBooks, 2018.

———. *School as a Journey: The Eight-Year Odyssey of a Waldorf Teacher and His Class.* Hudson, NY: Anthroposophic Press, 1995; also translated into several other languages.

———. *School Renewal: A Spiritual Journey for Change.* Hudson, NY: Anthroposophic Press, 1999. Spanish translation available: *Renovación escolar: Un viaje espiritual hacia el cambio.* Great Barrington, MA: SteinerBooks, 2014.

———. *A Second Classroom: Parent–Teacher Relationships in a Waldorf School*. Great Barrington, MA: SteinerBooks, 2014.

———. *Silence Is Complicity: A Call to Let Teachers Improve Our Schools through Action Research—Not NCLB*. Great Barrington, MA: SteinerBooks, 2007.

Floride, Athys. *Human Encounters and Karma*. Hudson, NY: Anthroposophic Press, 1983.

Glas, Norbert. *Reading the Face: Understanding a Person's Character through Physiognomy: A Spiritual-Scientific Study*. Forest Row, UK: Temple Lodge, 2008.

Goethe, Johann Wolfgang von. *The Fairy Tale of the Green Snake and the Beautiful Lily*. Stourbridge, UK: Wynstones Press, 2007.

Hartmann, Steffen. *The Michael Prophecy and the Years 2012–2033: Rudolf Steiner and the Culmination of Anthroposophy*. Forest Row, UK: Temple Lodge, 2020.

Jocelyn, John and Beredine Jocelyn. *The Beneficent Role of Destiny*. Spring Valley, NY: St. George Publications, 1983.

Mees, L. F. C. *Secrets of the Skeleton: Form in Metamorphosis*. Hudson, NY: Anthroposophic Press, 1995.

Muller, Wayne. *Sabbath: Finding Rest, Renewal, and Delight in Our Busy Lives*. New York: Bantam, 1999.

Querido, René. *Questions and Answers on Reincarnation & Karma*. Spring Valley, NY: St. George Publications, 1977.

Sadhguru. *Karma: A Yogi's Guide to Crafting Your Destiny*. Haryana, India: Penguin, 2021.

Steiner, Rudolf. *Awakening to Community* (CW 257). Spring Valley, NY: Anthroposophic Press, 1974.

———. *The Being of Man and His Future Evolution* (CW 107). London: Rudolf Steiner Press, 1981 (out of print); the current edition contains the complete lecture course of 18 lectures: see *Disease, Karma, and Healing*.

———. *Disease, Karma, and Healing: Spiritual-Scientific Enquiries into the Nature of the Human Being* (CW 107). Forest Row, UK: Rudolf Steiner Press, 2013.

Bibliography

———. *Esoteric Christianity and the Mission of Christian Rosenkreutz* (CW 130). Forest Row, UK: Rudolf Steiner Press, 2001; lecture, Feb. 8, 1912, "The True Attitude to Karma" (lecture previously published as "Facing Karma," Spring Valley, NY: Anthroposophic Press, 1975).

———. "Facing Karma," Spring Valley, NY: Anthroposophic Press, 1975 (currently contained in *Esoteric Christianity;* see above).

———. *The Fifth Gospel: From the Akashic Record* (CW 148). Forest Row, UK: Rudolf Steiner Press, 1985.

———. *The Foundations of Human Experience* (CW 293, 66). Hudson, NY: Anthroposophic Press, 1996.

———. *How to Know Higher Worlds: A Modern Path of Initiation* (CW 10). Hudson, NY: Anthroposophic Press, 1994.

———. *The Karma of Materialism: Aspects of Human Evolution* (CW 176). Spencertown, NY: SteinerBooks, 2022.

———. *The Karma of Untruthfulness: Secret Societies, the Media, and Preparations for the Great War,* 2 vols. (CW 173, 174). Forest Row, UK: Rudolf Steiner Press, 2005.

———. *Karmic Relationships: Esoteric Studies,* 8 vols. (CW 235–240). London: Rudolf Steiner Press, 1972–1985.

———. *Manifestations of Karma* (CW 120). London: Rudolf Steiner Press, 1996.

———. *An Outline of Esoteric Science* (CW 13). Hudson, NY: Anthroposophic Press, 1997.

———. *Reincarnation and Karma: Two Fundamental Truths of Human Existence* (CW 135). Great Barrington, MA: Anthroposophic Press, 2001.

———. *Understanding Healing: Meditative Reflections on Deepening Medicine through Spiritual Science* (CW 316). Great Barrington, MA: SteinerBooks, 2013.

———. *A Western Approach to Reincarnation and Karma: Selected Lectures and Writings by Rudolf Steiner* (edited and introduced by René Querido). Hudson, NY: Anthroposophic Press, 1997.

Steiner, Rudolf, and Ita Wegman. *Extending Practical Medicine: Fundamental Principles Based on the Science of Spirit* (CW 27). Forest Row, UK: Rudolf Steiner Press, 1997.

Talbott, Steve. *Extraordinary Lives: Disability and Destiny in a Technological Age.* Ghent, NY: The Nature Institute, 2003.

Van Houten, Coenraad. *Practising Destiny: Principles and Processes in Adult Learning.* London: Temple Lodge, 2000.

Waldorf Leadership and Community Development Program

Cultivate your capacity to serve in leadership positions

This highly-regarded Waldorf Leadership and Community Development Program (WLCD) is designed to support independent and public Waldorf school administrators, staff, trustees, parents, and pedagogical leaders to develop, expand, and deepen group and leadership skills.

This is a 10-month online and low-residency program with virtual, interactive courses and 2 residencies with our stellar guest presenters.

Choose your pathway

1) Full program with all virtual seminars and two f2f weekend residencies earns a WLCD program graduation certificate.
2) All virtual seminars and courses (no f2f residencies) earns a certificate of online participation.

The program includes workshops, guided exercises, case studies, mentoring, and presentations in areas such as group dynamics, role clarity, communication, conflict resolution, navigating change efforts, strategic vs. tactical decision making, community development, and collaborative leadership among other topics brought by a great line-up of guest presenters.

Center for Anthroposophy
Waldorf Teacher Education, Renewal & Research

Torin Finser, Ph.D., Program Director
Karen Atkinson, Program Coordinator
Office: (603) 654-2566
Web: bit.ly/wlcd_program

Image: KMF

www.ingramcontent.com/pod-product-compliance
Lightning Source LLC
Chambersburg PA
CBHW071933160426
43198CB00011B/1375